Praise for *Breaking the Silence Habit*

"The essential workplace guide for the #MeToo era. Powerful tools for managers and employees wrestling with big, uncomfortable questions. Sarah's book will help people become happier, more fulfilled, and less anxious at work."

—**Morra Aarons-Mele, founder of Women Online, bestselling author of** *Hiding in the Bathroom*, **and host of** *Harvard Business Review*'s *The Anxious Achiever*

"Sarah brings a practical tool kit and warm wisdom that will directly improve leaders' ability to bring out the best in their teams in the #MeToo era. A must-read for leaders."

—**Rebecca Towne, CEO, Vermont Electric Company**

"Packed full of useful tips and tools, *Breaking the Silence Habit* offers a fresh take on approaching sexual harassment in organizations—one that multiplies the effects of compliance-based policies."

—**Toyin Ajayi, M.D., Physician and Entrepreneur**

"In a world that dances around uncomfortable conversations, Beaulieu's book takes us right to the belly of the beast—where real change is made with courage, vulnerability, and heart."

—**Haley Hoffman Smith, author of** *Her Big Idea*

"Finally, a must-read practical road map for leaders to eliminate workplace sexual harassment in the #MeToo era."

—**Saul Kaplan, founder and Chief Catalyst, Business Innovation Factory, and author of** *The Business Model Innovation Factory*

"Respectfully written, grounded in best practice, and mindful not to place blame or shame, *Breaking the Silence Habit* transforms the reader . . . Teaching these concepts in schools today can help foster a healthier workplace for our children's future."

—**Judy LoBianco, 2018 Education Week Leader to Learn From; Past-President, Society of Health and Physical Educators; and CEO, HPE Solutions, LLC**

"Sarah Beaulieu calls us to action in a digestible way and brings clarity to a complicated and historically underdiscussed topic. A must-read for public servants grappling with how to talk about sexual misconduct with more nuance and grace."

—**Bo Machayo, Chief of Staff and Chair at Large, Loudoun County (Virginia) Board of Supervisors, and former White House official**

"If we're going to change the world, we have to be willing to change the conversation. And to do that, we must get comfortable with getting messy first. Sarah has made the messy part easier to navigate in a way that is approachable, whip-smart—and most importantly, effective."

—Jennifer Iannolo, founder of Global Innovation Incubator for Women and featured expert, US State Department

"Sarah is uniquely positioned to write this quintessential guide to having uncomfortable conversations in the #MeToo workplace. She gives us a practical framework and tools to have those important conversations. Get ready to be uncomfortable! Your family, friends, and work colleagues will thank you for it."

—Jeffrey Saviano, Global Professional Service Firm Innovation Leader, MIT Connection Science Fellow, and host of the *Better Innovation* podcast

"In *Breaking the Silence Habit*, Sarah delivers an indispensable guide to the power of conversation in the prevention of sexual harassment in the workplace. A must-read for practitioners facing these critical issues in their own companies."

—Kate Murtagh, Chief Compliance Officer, Harvard Management Company

"Beaulieu has done something quite impressive with this book; she's deconstructed an incredibly complex and fraught topic to provide practical advice on how we can all have tough conversations. This book isn't just for women—or for men. It's for all who care about having a safe, inclusive culture at their organization. Beaulieu's expertise on this topic is evident in these pages. She's given us not only an inclusive, practical way to tackle sensitive topics but also a road map for changing the organizational cultures that often keep us silent. A much-needed book at the exact right time."

—Amy Gallo, author of *HBR Guide to Dealing with Conflict*

"Sarah's is an authoritative and essential voice that will help all entrepreneurs find theirs as they develop new ventures with new cultures. Because more than ever entrepreneurial success relies on successful teams, entrepreneurs must communicate honestly—especially about uncomfortable topics. Sarah and *Breaking the Silence Habit* are indispensable resources in any entrepreneurial journey."

—Danny Warshay, Executive Director, Nelson Center for Entrepreneurship, Brown University

BREAKING THE SILENCE HABIT

BREAKING THE
SILENCE
HABIT

A PRACTICAL GUIDE TO
UNCOMFORTABLE CONVERSATIONS
IN THE #METOO WORKPLACE

SARAH BEAULIEU

BK
Berrett–Koehler Publishers, Inc.

Berrett-Koehler Publishers, Inc.
1333 Broadway, Suite 1000, Oakland, CA 94612-1921
Tel: (510) 817-2277   Fax: (510) 817-2278   www.bkconnection.com

ORDERING INFORMATION
Quantity sales. Special discounts are available on quantity purchases by corporations, associations, and others. For details, contact the "Special Sales Department" at the Berrett-Koehler address above.

Individual sales. Berrett-Koehler publications are available through most bookstores. They can also be ordered directly from Berrett-Koehler: Tel: (800) 929-2929; Fax: (802) 864-7626; www.bkconnection.com.

Orders for college textbook / course adoption use. Please contact Berrett-Koehler: Tel: (800) 929-2929; Fax: (802) 864-7626.

Distributed to the U.S. trade and internationally by Penguin Random House Publisher Services.

Berrett-Koehler and the BK logo are registered trademarks of Berrett-Koehler Publishers, Inc.

Printed in the United States of America

Berrett-Koehler books are printed on long-lasting acid-free paper. When it is available, we choose paper that has been manufactured by environmentally responsible processes. These may include using trees grown in sustainable forests, incorporating recycled paper, minimizing chlorine in bleaching, or recycling the energy produced at the paper mill.

Library of Congress Cataloging-in-Publication Data
Names: Beaulieu, Sarah, author.
Title: Breaking the silence habit : a practical guide to uncomfortable
  conversations in the #MeToo workplace / Sarah Beaulieu.
Description: First edition. | Oakland, CA : Berrett-Koehler Publishers,
  [2020] | Includes bibliographical references and index.
Identifiers: LCCN 2019050004 | ISBN 9781523087402 (paperback ; alk. paper)
  | ISBN 9781523087419 (pdf) | ISBN 9781523087426 (epub)
Subjects: LCSH: Sexual harassment. | Sex in the workplace. | Violence in
  the workplace. | Organizational behavior.
Classification: LCC HD6060.3 .B43 2020 | DDC 305.42--dc23
LC record available at https://lccn.loc.gov/2019050004

First Edition   26 25 24 23 22 21 20   10 9 8 7 6 5 4 3 2 1

Produced by Wilsted & Taylor | Text design by Nancy Koerner | Copy editing by Nancy Evans
Cover design by Irene Morris Design

Note: This book does not provide professional legal advice or opinions. The stories and anecdotes in this book are all based on real-life incidents and conversations, but names and details have been changed to protect privacy.

To Marc, Maryellen, and Russ

CONTENTS

FOREWORD by Len Schlesinger ... xi

PREFACE ... xiii

PART I. GETTING STARTED

START HERE

WHY WE NEED MORE UNCOMFORTABLE CONVERSATIONS AT WORK ... 3

Imagining a Workplace of the Future ... 3

▶ **GLOSSARY OF TERMS** ... 4

The Value of an Uncomfortable
 Conversation ... 6

Breaking the Silence Habit in
 Today's Workplace ... 9

What You'll Learn and Why It Matters ... 11

A Special Note for and about Survivors
 of Sexual Abuse and Assault ... 15

▶ **GET HELP IF YOU NEED IT** ... 15

CHAPTER 1

A SKILLS-BASED APPROACH TO SEXUAL HARASSMENT PREVENTION AND RESPONSE ... 17

Skills vs. Rules ... 17

A Step-by-Step Approach for Teams
 and Organizations ... 20

The Rationale behind a Skills-Based Approach ... 26

CHAPTER 2

YOUR CONVERSATION EXPERIENCE
AND WHY IT MATTERS ... 29

CASE STUDY **SHOULDN'T THIS BE OBVIOUS?** ... 30

The Challenges and Opportunities of
Diverse Experience ... 31

Introducing the Conversation Experience Assessment
to Your Team ... 33

CONVERSATION EXPERIENCE ASSESSMENT ... 35

PART II. THE UNCOMFORTABLE
CONVERSATION FRAMEWORK

CHAPTER 3

KNOW THE FACTS ... 43

Why Use a Framework? ... 43

Facts You May Not Know ... 45

Staying Open to Facts ... 48

The Role of Facts in Uncomfortable
Conversations ... 50

CHAPTER 4

GET UNCOMFORTABLE ... 55

The Inevitability of Discomfort ... 55

How to Respond to Discomfort ... 59

CHAPTER 5

PAUSE THE REACTION ... 65

Why Take a Pause? ... 65

How to Get Curious, Not Furious ... 65

▶ **TO THOSE WHO ARE UNDERSTANDABLY ANGRY** ... 68

Big Reactions, Big Pauses . . . 70

The Blame Game . . . 73

▶ A PAUSE FOR MALE SURVIVORS . . . 74

CHAPTER 6

EMBRACE PRACTICAL QUESTIONS . . . 77

What Is a Practical Question? . . . 77

The Art of Asking . . . 79

What If I Get Called Out? . . . 82

CHAPTER 7

SEE THE WHOLE PICTURE . . . 85

The Whole Incident Picture . . . 85

The Whole Gender Picture . . . 89

The Whole Survivor Picture . . . 90

The Framework in Action . . . 93

PART III. PUTTING CONVERSATIONS
INTO PRACTICE

CHAPTER 8

THE POWER OF PRACTICE . . . 101

Choosing Conversation over Silence . . . 101

The How and Why of Practice Conversations . . . 103

CASE STUDY **THE NAKED MUD WRESTLING VIDEO** . . . 106

Skills Gained through Practice . . . 110

CHAPTER 9

HELPFUL INTERVENTION . . . 113

Understanding Impact and Intervention . . . 113

Tips for Effective Intervention . . . 117

▶ I SAW SOMETHING. WHAT DO I SAY?. . . 118

PRACTICE CONVERSATION #1:
   INAPPROPRIATE COMMENTS . . . 119

PRACTICE CONVERSATION #2:
   NOT TAKING TRAINING SERIOUSLY . . . 121

CHAPTER 10

POWER AND BOUNDARIES . . . 125

Recognizing and Addressing Power . . . 125

PRACTICE CONVERSATION #3:
   POWER DYNAMICS AND HARASSMENT . . . 127

Setting and Respecting Boundaries . . . 129

PRACTICE CONVERSATION #4:
   DISPLAY OF AFFECTION . . . 134

PRACTICE CONVERSATION #5:
   UNCLEAR BOUNDARIES AND COMMUNICATION . . . 136

CHAPTER 11

RESPONDING TO DISCLOSURES
AND SUPPORTING SURVIVORS . . . 139

Responding to a Report of Sexual
   Harassment or Assault . . . 139

Before You Get Started: Key Issues Impacting Disclosures
   and Reports . . . 144

PRACTICE CONVERSATION #6:
   OBSTACLES TO REPORTING . . . 145

CASE STUDY **MY COLLEAGUE WAS ASSAULTED
   AND NEEDS SUPPORT** . . . 147

Understanding the Impact of Sexual Abuse
   and Assault on the Workplace . . . 151

PRACTICE CONVERSATION #7:
   SURVIVORS AT WORK . . . 153

CHAPTER 12

PRACTICE AND HABITS ... 157

How to Keep the Conversations Going ... 157

Nine-Week Manager-Led Conversation Plan ... 157

Habits for Managers ... 163

Action Steps for Individuals ... 164

Start an Uncomfortable Conversation Group ... 166

CHAPTER 13

NAVIGATING COMMON
CONVERSATION CHALLENGES ... 169

Can I date my colleague? ... 169

Should I just avoid people who aren't my gender? ... 171

What if my friends are jerks? ... 172

How do I assess my own behavior? ... 174

I've been harassed. What do I do? ... 176

CONCLUSION

TYING IT ALL TOGETHER ... 179

NOTES ... 181

ACKNOWLEDGMENTS ... 185

INDEX ... 187

ABOUT THE AUTHOR ... 196

FOREWORD

This is an important book about a difficult topic. All around us we are connecting to stories about sexual assault. Some are sharing decades-old stories, sometimes for the first time. Others are speaking out publicly, licensed by the current setting of #MeToo coverage. In the news we read or watch, and increasingly in the courts, it's impossible to avoid these stories and the conversations about them. But from my vantage point, there does not appear to be much progress in improving the quality or the outcomes of these efforts at "voice."

As president of Babson College, I tried to hire Sarah to work for me. While I was unsuccessful in this attempt, I nonetheless stayed connected to her and her work and have benefited enormously from that connection. Over the years, Sarah has frequently spoken to me about her desire to address the paralyzing effect sexual assault and harassment has on the ability of people to cross the threshold of difficult and uncomfortable conversations at work, at school, at home, and among families, friends, and lovers.

A few years ago, during a career transition, she simply got started. Over the last decade, I've watched her apply her skills as a fund-raiser for nonprofits, a first-rate strategist for social enterprises, a wife, and a mother. I am impressed with the skills she brings to all that she tackles in the world.

Sarah began by speaking publicly to a broad array of groups, quickly discovering that all the people she engaged with indicated profound uncertainty and discomfort discussing the topic in almost any circumstance. These talks provided evidence both that she had something to say and that very few others were attempting to address the role of conversations themselves. The law of large numbers—from her speeches, side conversations, consulting, and training—has allowed Sarah to see patterns emerge. She has now collapsed the conversations and her experiences into a practical methodology for those of us avoiding these chats to begin, to practice, and ultimately to become competent and comfortable with what she calls "uncomfortable conversations." There is little doubt that the world will be a much better place if we begin this work now.

This is what brings us to *Breaking the Silence Habit*. Whether you are simply trying to build your own capabilities in holding "uncomfortable conversations" or you lead or support an organization trying to build these competencies on a broader scale, Sarah has provided you with a valuable guide to the work that you have before you. I hope that, like me, you finish reading the book ready to get started, to practice, and to get comfortable with uncomfortable conversations!

LEN SCHLESINGER
Baker Foundation Professor, Harvard Business School
President Emeritus, Babson College

A PERSONAL AND PROFESSIONAL
JOURNEY IN CONVERSATIONS

My first conversation about sexual violence took place when I was eleven years old. It was the night I told my mom that a family member was molesting me. We were visiting a relative's home in Oregon, and something terrible happened. It wasn't the first time—or the last time—I was sexually abused or assaulted. But it was the first time I spoke about it out loud.

I remember the conversation as though it happened yesterday. The look of shock on my mom's face. The fact that she believed me instantly. My parents' muffled voices in the next room, arguing. The next morning, we ate breakfast. There was some kind of confrontation with the abuser. We stayed the rest of our visit. The discomfort was palpable. It felt like mud in the air.

I learned a lot about the power of conversations during that visit to Oregon. I learned that a single conversation can change the direction of our lives. I learned that conversations about sexual violence are always and inherently difficult and uncomfortable. I learned that undoing generational habits of silence requires constant attention to both the conversations we have and the ones we avoid.

By believing my story, my mom helped lay the first stone on what would become a long cobblestone pathway to healing.

However, it did not immediately undo the damage of being sexually abused. In the aftermath of that Oregon visit, I struggled with depression, self-hatred, an eating disorder, and even thoughts of taking my own life.

Little by little, step by step, stone by stone, conversation by conversation, my healing started to unfold. The therapist who asked the right questions and believed in my capacity to heal. My best male friend who fought the pressure to fix and instead learned to simply sit with me when I cried. The acquaintance who didn't change the subject when I mentioned being molested. The date who told me I didn't deserve what happened to me, and took extra care to approach intimacy safely. The colleague who asked me more about the rape crisis center where I volunteered, and the bosses who didn't blink an eye when I took an hour for therapy appointments during lunch. Each conversation laid down a stone, and eventually I found my way to a sense of resilience and wholeness most survivors of sexual abuse don't get to find.

My personal experience as a survivor, and gratitude for my healing, sparked a passion for creating cobblestone pathways for other survivors, and for people who want to help them but don't always know how. Every conversation I could now spark with a friend, date, colleague, boss, or stranger laid down a stone not just for me but also for others who might walk the same path. My passion for inspiring and having these valuable conversations was— and is—grounded in an almost obsessive optimism about humans and the world, an unending thirst to listen and learn, and a sense of obligation to pay the world back for the healing I found through luck, privilege, and grace.

These characteristics led me a degree in women's studies and to numerous volunteer roles as a crisis counselor working with and alongside survivors of sexual violence. In college, I worked equally with fraternities and feminist groups, once bringing disparate campus groups together to respond meaningfully to an incident of rape. The fraternity council, bewildered by the incident, initially balked at the idea of a rally outside the fraternity where an off-campus party guest had assaulted a female student. In the heat of the moment, the women organizing the rally took their objection as victim-blaming. After speaking with representatives from both groups, we came up with a meaningful alternative: a candlelight vigil with active participation from the fraternities. Listening to these young men choke up at the idea that someone was harmed at their event moved me deeply, and their vulnerability provided a much-needed moment of healing on campus—for everyone.

After graduation, I moved into a house with six male rowers, where I spent many nights listening and talking with a bunch of guys about the various pressures of gender, relationships, and sex, often over beers. The topics we talked about ranged from how women worked hard to stay safe at parties to the precautions my friends took when walking home at night to the time-intensive work spent on healing and recovery, and the role male friends played. I gained new insights into the challenges men face around empathy, intimacy, and connection, and how tricky it can be to communicate across genders. I learned how deep their desire was to support the women in their lives, and how little education and support they received to do so skillfully.

Over the years, my professional life has helped me build further skills to facilitate conversations among different kinds of individuals and groups. As a fund-raiser, strategist, and consultant, I've had opportunities to immerse myself in the perspectives of liberals and conservatives, individuals with wealth and without, corporate and community leaders, and the young and the old—groups who frequently approach similar missions in very different ways. As a volunteer and board member for a rape crisis center, I reflected on the obstacles many survivors face around healing and immersed myself deeply in the existing and emerging efforts around sexual violence prevention and response.

Together, these personal and professional experiences have led me to the central message of this book: uncomfortable conversations are worth having. An uncomfortable conversation is an activity that all of us can do. It's also a skill, one that we can learn even if we've never done it before, and one that we can master if we're interested in doing so. Being skilled at having uncomfortable conversations is a way of being in the world, a cornerstone habit of healthy people and cultures.

To create a world free of sexual harassment and violence, we need cobblestone pathways at home, in schools, and in our workplaces. These are pathways we can build together, stone by stone, conversation by conversation. My hope is that this book will provide leaders, managers, and employees with the tools they need to begin carving workplace pathways toward cultures of resilience and safety—pathways paved with the uncomfortable conversations we will have with ourselves, our teams, and our colleagues. May this book be a place where your questions are answered without judgment, you can learn without shame, and you'll be met where you are.

GETTING STARTED

WHY WE NEED MORE UNCOMFORTABLE CONVERSATIONS AT WORK

IMAGINING A WORKPLACE OF THE FUTURE

If 25 percent of your organization's employees suffered from diabetes, how would your organization adapt? Likely, diabetes management and prevention would become a theme across onboarding, management training, and internal communications. Healthy eating and exercise might be a central theme of your organization's outings and meetings. All of your bathrooms would have disposal containers for needles, and you might have a corporate discount for insulin pumps. You'd be trained on how to recognize and respond to signs that someone's blood sugar might be too high or too low. You'd expect company chatter to include tips about controlling diabetes, the best doctors, and new innovations. Every year, your company would participate in Diabetes Awareness Month and make a huge contribution to research. As someone with diabetes, you'd feel safe and supported at work. The investments your organization made in diabetes would have positive benefits for everyone in the company.

In the wake of the #MeToo movement, employees and leaders are coming to terms with the pervasiveness of sexual harassment within their organizations and industries and are struggling with the right ways to respond.[1] Depending on the industry or

> ▶ **GLOSSARY OF TERMS**
>
> *Sexual Violence* According to the Centers for Disease Control and Prevention, sexual violence is "a sexual act that is committed or attempted by another person without freely given consent of the victim or against someone who is unable to consent or refuse. It includes: forced or alcohol/drug facilitated penetration of a victim; forced or alcohol/drug facilitated incidents in which the victim was made to penetrate a perpetrator or someone else; nonphysically pressured unwanted penetration; intentional sexual touching; or noncontact acts of a sexual nature."[2]
>
> *Sexual Harassment* Legally, sexual harassment is discrimination based on sex that violates Title VII of the Civil Rights Act of 1964. The Equal Employment Opportunity Commission defines sexual harassment as "unwelcome sexual advances, requests for sexual favors, and other verbal or physical conduct of a sexual nature." Further, the behavior is only legally considered sexual harassment if it impacts, directly or indirectly, "an individual's employment, unreasonably interferes with an individual's work performance, or creates an intimidating, hostile, or offensive work environment."[3]

company, reported rates of sexual harassment range from 25 to 85 percent.[4] Without safety, work is made more challenging. Whether harassment consists of physical touching, direct comments about appearance or sexuality, or a culture where people are objectified, the conditions that permit sexual harassment leave workers in a state of vigilance that precludes them from bringing their full talent and contributions to the workplace. At the same time, working in a volatile climate where people are afraid to ask questions and learn new behaviors also inhibits efforts to prevent sexual harassment and establish positive and productive ways of working together. A 2018 study by the Pew Research Center found that the increased focus on sexual harassment and assault has made it harder for 51 percent of male respondents to know how to interact with women in the workplace.[5] And in the midst of this, many of those who have already experienced sexual abuse or assault—one in three women,[6] one in six men,[7] and one in two transgender individuals[8]—still show up at work with parts of their identities hidden from view.

Imagine, for a moment, a gender-diverse workplace where these things are not true. Sexual harassment doesn't take place. People of all genders safely and confidently interact with one another. What are the characteristics of an environment where

GLOSSARY OF TERMS, *cont.*

Sexual Abuse, Assault, and Misconduct Throughout this book, you will also see other terms—such as sexual abuse, sexual assault, and sexual misconduct—as reminders that we are talking about both verbal comments and physical acts of touching across a spectrum of aggression and violence. While the terms "sexual violence" and "sexual harassment" technically include both comments of a sexual nature and unwanted sexual contact, they are terms that people outside of public health or the legal profession interpret in different ways.

What to Call People Who Experience Sexual Harassment or Violence Some people who experience sexual violence call themselves victims and others call themselves survivors. Some people call themselves people who experienced sexual abuse or assault. In this book, you will see these terms used interchangeably.

people of all genders feel safe and can therefore bring their full productivity to bear on their roles? It's a place where people can talk about workplace relationships. It's a place where power is something that can be seen and discussed openly. It's a place where people set and respect boundaries, and discuss them when there is a difference in approach. It's a place where people receive feedback or experience conflict, integrate what they've learned, and go back to work. It's a place where people look out for one another and share responsibility not just for the work they do, but for how they do it together.

We can't attain this future workplace of safety and productivity through rules alone. We're also going to need to develop new skills around boundaries, behavior, and relationships. These skills certainly aren't easy to master, but they are skills we can learn ourselves and help to teach others.

THE VALUE OF AN UNCOMFORTABLE CONVERSATION

All of these skills have one central thing in common: a willingness to engage in conversations many of us find uncomfortable. The skill of engaging in an uncomfortable conversation—and an organizational habit built around it—is at the core of unlocking a future where people of all genders can work together in safe and productive ways.

What defines an uncomfortable conversation? It's a conversation where we intentionally prioritize the safety and health of our relationships and our community, even if it means making ourselves feel uncomfortable. The conversations themselves may look different for each of us, depending on our personal and cultural backgrounds, our gender, our professional experiences, and our individual personalities. Many of us don't realize, or perhaps don't want to admit, when a conversation makes us uncomfortable, and that complicates things still more—especially if we want to appear cool, professional, or calm in front of others. When it comes to sexual harassment, we bump up against many underlying topics that are inherently uncomfortable, including coming face-to-face with the reality of sexual abuse and assault.

When we learn to recognize opportunities for these conversations and develop the skill to engage in them, uncomfortable conversations about sexual harassment and misconduct can benefit relationships, organizations, and communities. For instance, when my son was seven years old, he asked if he could google something on my phone. After I PROMISED not to change my face when he told me what it was, he whispered in my ear, "naked girls."

I was a little confused. "You've seen your sister naked, so what exactly are you trying to see?"

"Well, I just want to see A LOT of them."

Was I uncomfortable? Of course. This was a new kind of conversation for me to have with my son, and my discomfort was amplified still more by the fact that I'm a survivor of sexual abuse and assault. Part of me wanted to run from the room.

Instead, I took a deep breath and logged onto my favorite sex-education site so that he could watch a few age-appropriate animated videos about male and female anatomy. Afterward, my son looked at me and said, "Well, I still want to see PICTURES of naked girls."

Oh, goodness. Were we talking about pornography, now? I hadn't prepared myself for this conversation, and scrambled to come up with a good angle. Since he's private about his own body, I simply asked if he'd want other people to find a naked photo of him on the Internet. The answer was an obvious no. We agreed it would not be cool if we could find pictures of other naked kids on the Internet, either.

I was proud of my son for being curious, and proud of him for asking such insightful questions—and told him so. I also let him know that there's a lot of wrong information on the Internet about bodies and sex, and if we google something like "naked girls," we might not get the right answer.

This comment resonated immediately, because he doesn't want to be a dummy about this topic, any more than he wants to be a dummy about Pokemon or the running speed of a cheetah.

I wrapped up the conversation by telling him that his friends are probably going to find incorrect information online, and might even share it with him. When that happens, he can always come to me to get smart about it.

Later in the book, I'll introduce you to the five-part Uncomfortable Conversation Framework and dive more deeply into both the benefits and characteristics of conversations like this one. The bottom line is that, by engaging more deeply in this uncomfortable conversation with my son rather than avoid it or shut it down, we both reaped key benefits.

- We established the trust and confidence that we could talk about uncomfortable things. The ice was now broken, and it was a lot easier for either of us to bring up the topic again.

- Both my son and I can pay the conversation forward. Now that I have—and am willing to share—this story, you can have a reference point for a similar conversation. You now know that if your child can spell, it's time to have a conversation about Internet safety. Even if you'd do it differently—better, I hope!—the subject is not brand-new.

- My son is now equipped to talk to peers about bodies, Internet safety, and why naked pictures don't belong online. His friends may or may not have similar conversations with their parents at home. But, even if they don't, they will benefit from having a peer who had this one conversation with his mom.

BREAKING THE SILENCE HABIT IN TODAY'S WORKPLACE

What is an uncomfortable conversation in the context of workplace sexual harassment? It's a conversation that requires us to acknowledge that our workplace is impacted by sexual harassment, abuse, and assault and that we are willing to help change it, even if it makes us feel uncomfortable. For some, it's a conversation that requires us to take accountability for laughing at jokes we didn't think were funny. For others, it's a conversation that requires us to wrestle with what to do when we're sexually attracted to a colleague. It's a conversation that forces us to consider personal upbringing and histories in the context of work. It's a conversation that might cause us to consider our behaviors, boundaries, relationships, or reactions in new ways.

When we don't know how someone will react, or can't predict the outcome of an uncomfortable conversation, it sometimes seems easier to avoid the topic altogether, doesn't it? There's just one problem with that solution: if we all stay silent because we're uncomfortable, nothing will ever change.

What if, instead of avoiding uncomfortable conversations about sexual harassment and violence, we could simply get better at having them? When we embrace uncomfortable conversations as a skill and as a practice, we can break the cycle of avoidance and silence that leaves us all feeling unstable and unsafe.

When we talk about sexual harassment and violence, we may be forced to confront competing truths about the world that we hold at a very deep level. Regardless of the reason, the process of shifting our mindset is the same. To engage in a conversation about sexual harassment and violence, we first have to expect to feel uncomfortable. The discomfort isn't a sign that we're doing it wrong—it's a sign that we're doing it at all. When we feel uncomfortable in a conversation, remember that we are choosing the discomfort that produces positive results, not just for us but also for the communities and cultures in which we live and work.

Gender diversity in the workplace is not going away. The #MeToo movement is not going away. If organizations are to achieve the psychological—and physical—safety required for productivity,[9] they must establish new ways of behaving and interacting among employees. This requires people of all genders to learn new skills, not just hear about the same rules, more forcefully stated. Without a new approach to sexual harassment prevention and response, organizations will continue to face financial, legal, and reputational repercussions.

How do we establish new ways of behaving and interacting? We must first break the core habit that contributes to the prevalence of sexual harassment in the first place: silence. If we are silent, we are not speaking up when we see or hear something we know or suspect is wrong. Instead, we are signaling to perpetrators that their behavior is acceptable to us, even if it isn't. If we are silent, we are not speaking up in ways that make survivors of sexual abuse or assault feel safe and supported at work. Being silent prevents us from learning whether our workplace interactions are contributing to safety and respect for our teams and organizations.

When it comes to sexual harassment and violence, choosing silence over conversation is a deeply embedded habit for both individuals and organizations. We don't know what to say. We aren't sure we'll get it right and are terrified of getting it wrong. We feel helpless and overwhelmed. We don't want to face the reality of the pervasiveness and impact of the problem. The moment comes and goes. The good news is that habits are replaceable, and by replacing a habit of silence with a habit of uncomfortable conversation, it's then possible to develop more skill in creating professional boundaries and relationships, intervening in a helpful way, and responding to and supporting those in your community who experience sexual harassment and violence.

At work, we need to do more than simply avoid negative be-

havior. We need new and improved skills, not just stronger definitions and rules. We need a mindset to approach a difficult topic,
and a chance to practice new kinds of conversations. We need to
ask the right questions, not just be told one-size-fits-all answers.
We need to initiate uncomfortable conversations rather than
waiting for situations to implode. Our work together is to create
a workplace culture that embraces new habits of uncomfortable
conversation, not the old habits of silence.

WHAT YOU'LL LEARN AND WHY IT MATTERS

Breaking the Silence Habit is a practical guide for leaders, managers, and employees who want their workplaces to feel safer and
less volatile in the #MeToo era and beyond. This book won't tell
you the right thing to say in every moment, but no matter what
role you play in your organization, it will provide you with practical ways that you can break the habits of silence that undermine
workplace productivity and safety.

The book begins by orienting you to a new way of thinking
about sexual harassment prevention and response, an approach
that moves beyond rules and reaction and into skills and prevention. Chapter 1, "A Skills-Based Approach to Sexual Harassment
Prevention and Response," kicks off with an exploration of the
true purpose of rules and policies around sexual harassment, and
how they lay the groundwork for effective skills-based work. Chapter 1 will also provide a step-by-step overview of the skills-based
approach and the rationale behind it.

Chapter 2, "Your Conversation Experience and Why It Matters," introduces a survey tool you can use to assess your own experience with uncomfortable conversations about sexual harassment
and violence; you can also use it with your team. This chapter also
illustrates how the diversity of conversation experience across
your team may require you to adjust your expectations about what

constitutes a meaningful conversation about sexual harassment or violence.

This preparation leads into the heart of the book in Part II, "The Uncomfortable Conversation Framework." This five-part framework will build your capacity to engage in more meaningful and productive conversations about sexual harassment and violence. Each of the five parts of the Framework is described in a separate chapter (see facing page). The Framework is less of a step-by-step approach, and more of a collection of tools that enable you to engage in conversations in service of the larger community and culture. With this carefully considered framework, it's possible to participate in—and lead—a range of conversations that help support workplaces that more effectively prevent and respond to sexual harassment. Even with a framework, it takes both skill and practice to get to the point that these conversations feel natural. But without a framework, conversations about sexual harassment and violence can feel risky—even dangerous—to the point that we continue to avoid them.

After a solid grounding in The Uncomfortable Conversation Framework, we turn our focus to its practical application in developing new workplace skills. Part III, "Putting Conversations into Practice," is designed to provide you with all the tools and practical information you'll need to break the silence habit in your workplace. Chapter 8, "The Power of Practice," provides an overview of the benefits of practice and how practice can help you develop new skills. You'll also see a case study to demonstrate how this might play out with a group or a team. The next three chapters provide an overview of three core skills that can be developed through practicing uncomfortable conversations: "Helpful Intervention" (Chapter 9), "Power and Boundaries" (Chapter 10), and "Responding to Disclosures and Supporting Survivors" (Chapter 11).

Chapter 12, "Practice and Habits," offers additional tools

The Uncomfortable Conversation Framework

KNOW THE FACTS (Chapter 3) discusses the value of using a Framework and elaborates the first element of the Framework. This chapter offers basic information on the prevalence and impact of sexual abuse, assault, and harassment, and illustrates ways in which facts can illuminate solutions and next steps when we take the time to learn them.

GET UNCOMFORTABLE (Chapter 4) explores the inevitability of discomfort that comes with talking about sexual harassment and violence, including the origins of the discomfort and strategies for moving through it without shutting down a conversation.

PAUSE THE REACTION (Chapter 5) introduces the idea of a curious pause as a tool in uncomfortable conversations that are frequently emotional and polarized—a tool that allows you to continue the conversation in a more productive manner.

EMBRACE PRACTICAL QUESTIONS (Chapter 6) provides ways to use questions as a tool to learn and convey facts, move through discomfort, unpack a reaction, and see the conversation through another perspective.

SEE THE WHOLE PICTURE (Chapter 7) illustrates how zooming out to get new perspectives helps us move conversations beyond a single incident, person, or experience. Chapter 7 closes with an example of how uncomfortable conversations help to break workplace habits of silence while building new skills you can use to prevent and respond to sexual harassment.

managers and employees can use to permanently break the silence habit by systematically integrating uncomfortable conversations into day-to-day practices at work. Chapter 13, "Navigating Common Conversation Challenges," addresses common challenges and questions that arise when implementing a skills-based approach to sexual harassment prevention and response. To name a few: *Have I behaved inappropriately in the past? Are workplace relationships out of the question? Should I even be alone at work with anyone of another gender?*

There's no way that a single book is going to cover everything you need to know or address every conversation you may have on this topic. Some readers want an overall strategy for battling perpetrators of all forms of sexual harassment or violence. Some imagine a rule book on behavior in the workplace. Others may be seeking the perfect policy manual, one that will prevent future incidents of sexual harassment.

We might make some progress on some of those, but the central benefit this book offers is a framework for effective communication about sexual harassment and misconduct, and how to apply it to key areas in your organization, no matter what your place is in it. It offers a broader perspective on how you—or anyone—can engage in workplace conversations about sexual harassment and misconduct in more meaningful and productive ways. By applying this conversation framework in your organization or team, you can begin to build the sense of safety and respect that is required for effective and productive work. And you can make more rapid progress on other goals related to sexual harassment prevention and response.

My biggest hope is that, after reading this book and implementing these strategies, you'll be able to join me in creating a world where we've broken our habit of silence and embraced a habit of uncomfortable but highly productive and meaningful conversations.

A SPECIAL NOTE FOR AND ABOUT
SURVIVORS OF SEXUAL ABUSE AND ASSAULT

While written to serve workplaces, this book incorporates more than a few personal stories and anecdotes. This is intentional, and supports several key learning goals for individuals and organizations. First and foremost, sexual harassment is personal. Even when it happens at work, sexual harassment has profoundly personal implications. It brings up the same feelings of shame, stigma, and powerlessness that sexual abuse and assault cause in any other setting. Second, the conditions that permit sexual harassment to take place, including an avoidance of uncomfortable conversations, are often the same conditions that permit other kinds of sexual violence to take place in other arenas. When we break the silence about sexual abuse, we are also helping to break the silence that enables sexual harassment to take place. Third, we all must stand in solidarity with leaders, managers, and employees who have experienced sexual abuse or assault but may not share those experiences openly. Whether we know it or not, we all work with survivors of sexual abuse and assault. Conversations about workplace sexual harassment affect these survivors in ways we don't consider, unless personal experiences are allowed into the discussion.

For those of you who have personally survived sexual abuse or assault, please know that my personal stories are mine alone, as

> ▶ **GET HELP IF YOU NEED IT**
>
> In the United States, survivors can receive crisis support and referrals through the National Sexual Assault Hotline at 1-800-656-4673. Outside of the United States, many countries have national and local rape crisis centers or other hotlines, and crisis text services are accessible via an Internet search.

is my choice to share them. Your story may be different. You may want to share your experience at work, or you may never want to talk about it in the workplace. That decision is entirely up to you. I recognize the privileges I have in my healing, my professional experience, and my access to opportunity, which allow me to share this part of my life openly.

In my experience, being a survivor doesn't always make it easier to engage in meaningful and productive conversations about sexual harassment, especially in a workplace context. Personal histories can make the topic feel high-stakes, emotional, and volatile. Sometimes survivors hold back their experiences and expertise because they don't want to come out as survivors. In other cases, we lean into conversations in ways that leave us triggered, exhausted, and drained.

Please take care of yourself as you read this book, and as you engage in your own uncomfortable conversations in the workplace. The purpose of this book is to help make you and those around you more skilled at navigating these kinds of conversations, which will hopefully make your workplace safe and supportive. While my experience may not be the same as yours, I share it as a place to start the conversation. I hope you are reading this book with a glass of wine or a cup of tea—whatever contributes to your sense of self-care.

CHAPTER 1

A SKILLS-BASED APPROACH TO SEXUAL HARASSMENT PREVENTION AND RESPONSE

SKILLS VS. RULES

If our ultimate goal is to create gender-diverse workplaces that are safe and respectful, how might we go about ensuring that all employees both know the rules of the game and have the skills to follow them? Consider soccer for a moment. Let's say your goal is to get a group of diverse athletes and nonathletes to play a game of soccer together. How might you go about it?

You might start by explaining the rules of the game, allowable conduct on the field, and the penalties for breaking the rules. You might ask your team to read the rules in advance of the first practice and clarify any questions they might have. But it's pretty clear that talking about the rules of the game isn't the purpose or point of soccer practice.

To learn and master the game of soccer, you need to practice so you can build the skills of running, handling the ball on the field, and playing as a team. You need drills that people can practice alone and with each other. You need to learn the positions, and which one you are best suited to play. Some people will need to learn how to run while kicking a ball, while others will need to learn how to pass to others. Some people can run fast but can't shoot the ball, while others have great precision in their kicks, but can't get to the ball fast enough to take a shot. With regular practice and reminders of the rules of play, you might not win the World Cup, but you'd eventually be able to play a rewarding game of soccer.

When we hear the term "sexual harassment training," most of us think first and foremost about the rules part of training, also known as compliance. Compliance training typically consists of a review of the legal definitions of sexual harassment, company policy, and the repercussions for being in violation of company policy and the law. Sometimes this training will incorporate scenarios designed to teach participants how to recognize sexual harassment when it takes place. Sometimes the training will be offered as an online course, which saves companies money, but eliminates interactivity. The effectiveness of the training is measured in terms of completion rate and sometimes, in the case of online training, passing a test indicating that you understand the definitions and policies presented.

Compliance training evokes a wide range of reactions, and some training modules are still so poorly designed, it's hard to take them seriously. Recently, a friend of mine shared a slide from her company's compliance-focused online training module. Curious, I asked her what skills she was learning from the training. Her reply, in jest: speed-reading and multitasking.

A female human resources executive once shared with me that she left a compliance training early in her career feeling terrified and overwhelmed, telling herself she'd never touch anyone she worked with ever again. This is also a common reaction to a rules-based training. Employees of all genders often leave compliance trainings feeling frustrated that the trainings aren't useful or feeling scared, anxious, and fearful that their awkwardness or ignorance will result in losing their jobs.

These reactions are unfortunate, because compliance trainings play an important role in sexual harassment prevention. Rules do matter. They provide a common language for talking about behavior and set the expectation that those who commit sexual harassment will be held accountable. Compliance trainings also provide companies with the necessary legal mechanisms to hold perpetrators of sexual harassment accountable without being sued. Preventing lawsuits is important. If a company or organization is out of business, it can't pursue its mission or sustain its workforce.

Compliance is the perfect place to start. However, when training begins and ends with compliance, it creates challenges that can allow troubling behavior to continue. Oftentimes, compliance training leaves more questions than answers and doesn't support a tone or climate where those questions can be effectively answered and addressed.

Compliance doesn't always address power dynamics and boundary issues that are troubling, but not covered by policy. For instance, a man wondered whether the weekly poker night he hosted for his team was appropriate, given that the regular attendees were all men. Another man confided in me that his junior employee had stopped coming on sales calls with him after a compliance training, but he didn't know why.

"She avoids having even work-related conversations with me," he said. "I'm on eggshells, wondering if I did something wrong, but I'm afraid to ask her or bring it up with our district manager."

Even worse, perpetrators often aren't deterred by rules, even when those rules are clearly spelled out during compliance training. After all, sexual harassment was already against the rules before the #MeToo movement broke. When a perpetrator or potential perpetrator leaves a compliance training and returns to a culture of silence and avoidance, that sends a clear message that they can continue their behavior without repercussions.

Often people are made so uncomfortable during compliance training that they joke or laugh their way through it, or easily give the "right" answers and then revert to the status quo after training. Perpetrators of sexual harassment and misconduct thrive not only on the silence of their victims but also on the silence of bystanders. Perpetrators are enabled by a culture that doesn't collectively enforce the rules, and by individuals who don't share accountability for relationships and behavior at work.

A compliance training is not designed to create a more supportive environment for colleagues who may have experienced sexual abuse or assault. It's not a place where managers can learn how to better see the workplace through the eyes of survivors, or understand how their lived experience may affect boundaries and relationships with colleagues.

When it comes to compliance, the focus is on the kinds of behaviors to avoid and the consequences if we engage in them. For some, this evokes a type of fearful inaction, a reluctance to come anywhere near the topic again. For others, this evokes frustration, because the rules were already apparent to them. Regardless of these reactions, compliance is an essential first step.

If what we want in the workplace is a place where we have safer and more respectful relationships and interactions, we have to get on the playing field after learning the rules. When we understand that the rules are designed to set up a game that will be more fun for everyone, we're more likely to pay attention, ask questions, and actually follow the rules when we're playing the game.

A STEP-BY-STEP APPROACH
FOR TEAMS AND ORGANIZATIONS

Whether you are a CEO, a manager, or an entry-level professional, a broader approach to tackling sexual harassment will help you equip your team and colleagues with the necessary skills for today's workplace. You may be seeking to address interactions among your team members that are eroding trust and safety, or you may have witnessed troubling behavior, jokes, or comments.

You may see the limitations of compliance training, and want to do more in your department. You may be frustrated that your manager hasn't made a stronger commitment to preventing or responding to sexual harassment effectively, or feel deep empathy for those in your workplace who have experienced sexual harassment. You may be leading an organization-wide training initiative after a high-profile incident at the company or in the industry. Regardless of your reason for starting this work, it will help create more safety and respect in your workplace.

A skills-based approach to sexual harassment prevention and response incorporates five key steps.

STEP 1: Start with compliance, policy, and reporting

As outlined previously, there are several reasons to begin your skill development with compliance, company policy, and how reports of harassment will be handled. Whether a training is offered by your organization, as is required in several states, or it's something you learn on your own, consider this an opportunity to learn the rules of the game, why the rules exist, and what areas are subject to interpretation—and by whom. By asking questions about laws, policies, and reporting up front, you can ground yourself in the rules of the game before diving into a broader set of conversations that play a role in prevention and culture change.

If your company provides a compliance-based training, this first step is an opportunity to explore and discuss its purpose and limitations. If your company doesn't provide such a training, you can find decent ones online.

When you understand the role and purpose of compliance, it is a natural place to start the conversation about sexual harassment and misconduct with your colleagues or team. A discussion about compliance, policy, and reporting lays the groundwork for more meaningful conversations that explore prevention, culture, and the fuzziness around the edges of the rules. Take, for example, a situation where you saw another manager leaning over an intern to look at something on her computer screen, and he put his hand on her shoulder or back. Let's say you speak to your manager colleague about it, and he's offended. You used to think of him as a friend, but now he's giving you the cold shoulder and refuses to talk to you about it. He also joked with the intern about what you said, and now she seems annoyed with you, too. Did you do the wrong thing? Should you not have said anything about what you saw, even though your goal was to make the workplace safer for everyone? When we can differentiate between conversations about compliance and conversations about culture, it's easier to engage in both with more skill.

The first step of compliance training is also an important moment to make sure that you and your team understand the reporting process and are clear about the role of human resources in your organization. Demystifying and personalizing human resources helps set the stage for future uncomfortable conversations that may involve someone from that department. Many employees do not fully understand that human resources may impose disciplinary actions that fall short of firing someone and then, for legal reasons, can't discuss those outcomes. Others find the term "investigation" to be scary, when an investigation is really just a series of conversations involving someone from human resources, the person who made the report, the person who was mentioned in the report, and anyone who might have further information. In other words, an investigation is a series of uncomfortable conversations that are made even *more* uncomfortable when employees don't know their purposes or roles.

It's a lot easier to talk about the reporting process *before* there is an incident than it is to discuss it afterward. Once an incident has been reported, the process and outcome are typically kept confidential to protect all parties involved. This situation is uncomfortable for everyone. After an incident takes place, any discussion about the investigation or reporting process is more likely to sound insincere. If you aren't prepared to tolerate the ambiguity of an investigation and the lack of details about the outcome, it's easy to lose trust and make future conversations more difficult.

As a part of compliance discussions, it's helpful to provide insight into the questions your human resources team may grapple with on a daily basis. When do we give someone a chance to demonstrate accountability and growth? How do we properly document what we believe to be abusive behavior so we can legally terminate them—when no one wants to officially make a report? How can we conduct a fair and thorough investigation without making employees feel interrogated?

STEP 2: Assess experience in uncomfortable conversations

When it comes to sexual harassment, you are going to be engaging in conversations with people with a diverse range of experience and skill. Some employees will have experience addressing troubling behavior, responding to disclosures, or giving or receiving feedback. Many will not.

By reflecting on some very basic questions about your own history of conversations and the history of others, you can gain insights that will inform where your conversations may need more support or skill. For example, a group of employees who are surprised to hear sexual harassment takes place requires different practice conversations than a group that isn't at all surprised, but hasn't responded to reports in an official, professional capacity.

The mix of skill levels, however, is not the only challenge. The very fact that we are entering into these discussions with varied backgrounds, experiences, perspectives, and skills may surprise us. When a group conversation doesn't speak to our individual experiences or needs, we may end up feeling frustrated, annoyed, and distrustful of the process altogether.

By establishing a way of talking about and reflecting on experience at the outset of conversation practice, it's possible to manage expectations about the process, the cadence, and the reality that people will respond to the same situation in many different ways.

Whether initiating an informal discussion, integrating an exercise into training, or participating in the survey included in Chapter 2, ground the skills you seek to build in an actual assessment of experience.

STEP 3: Introduce The Uncomfortable Conversation Framework

Once these building blocks are in place, you can dive into The Uncomfortable Conversation Framework. The uncomfortable conversation is the foundational skill that makes the rest of this journey possible, which is why a significant portion of this book is dedicated to mapping out the Framework.

Through uncomfortable conversations, employees, managers, and leaders can develop the individual and organizational skills required to create safe and respectful work environments. For many people, an uncomfortable conversation might be any conversation about sexual harassment or violence, period. If you can't talk about sexual harassment or violence, you can't prevent or respond to it. The Framework will help you understand what to expect in a conversation about sexual harassment or violence and how to engage in one productively, regardless of someone's background or experience.

The Framework reflects five key insights gleaned from conversations with individuals from a range of backgrounds and experiences, as well as from experts in the field of sexual violence prevention and response. It offers a way for you to engage in many types of conversations about sexual harassment prevention and response, and helps you steer clear of the common traps that make these conversations polarizing or something to avoid.

Once you internalize the five parts of the Framework, you can start to use it more proactively to initiate uncomfortable conversations and use them to develop specific skills that support workplaces that prevent and respond to sexual harassment effectively. The Framework comes to life through practice, and the practice offers a chance to reinforce the Framework's core concepts.

Chapters 3 through 7 of this book provide an overview of the framework. If you are using this book to train a group or team, these chapters can be assigned as reading prior to a practice session, or you can find additional resources on my website, www.sarahbeaulieu.me, to help teach the Framework.

STEP 4: **Practice uncomfortable conversations**

After introducing the Framework, it's time to practice. The practice is the core of changing our habits, as it builds your skill, strengthens your ability to navigate behavior and relationships more effectively, and helps uncover potential policy or management issues within an organization or team.

Following the introduction of the Framework, I'll help you practice using realistic scenarios that you can use with trusted colleagues or in a facilitated group discussion with your team. These scenarios can be adapted to your industry and are designed to tackle some of the common roadblocks you and your organization may hit when trying to prevent or respond to sexual harassment.

These scenarios offer a chance to practice the skill of generating and engaging in productive, uncomfortable conversations. Practice also provides a chance to build new skills, such as helpful intervention, responding to a disclosure, supporting survivors at work, understanding power dynamics, and setting or respecting boundaries. Chapters 9, 10, and 11 will provide an overview of these key skills, why they matter, and how practice conversations can contribute to culture change in powerful ways.

STEP 5: **Build habits individually and through teams**

Avoiding conversations about sexual harassment and violence is an embedded habit for organizations and individuals. It will take intentional, active efforts to undo that habit and replace it with one of conversation. It's easy to attend a workshop, read a book, or respond to a conversation that someone else started. It's a lot harder to start one yourself. This requires more than a single practice conversation or even a single group practice session. However, it's the only way you and your team can move from responding to incidents after they happen to preventing them before they occur. The more you can commit to formalized uncomfortable conversations, the better chance you will have to change your own habits and the habits of your organization or team.

While some of the topics or methods presented here may feel forced, they are designed to help you break the ice in your role before an incident arises. Chapter 12 provides you with a series of habit-forming resources, no matter what your role is within your organization.

THE RATIONALE BEHIND A SKILLS-BASED APPROACH

There are three main reasons to adopt a skills-based approach. First, it builds on widely respected research into how organizations change. Second, it includes successful methods of changing behavior through replacing bad or ineffective habits. Third, it embraces common-sense philosophies about teaching and learning.

The basic tenets of change management reflect two core conditions required for organizations to change: a dissatisfaction with the status quo and a clear vision for the future.[1] When we don't shy away from speaking to the dissatisfaction of the current workplace across gender, we can unite around a process for change. A vision for the future is a gender-diverse workplace where we can engage in the kinds of conversations at work that support safe, respectful, and productive workplaces.

Recognizing that silence is often a habit enables us to leverage Charles Duhigg's research on habits to inform our approach to change. A habit of silence can therefore be replaced with a habit of speaking up. Changing core habits like this one requires building belief and trust in the vision that the world will be better as a result of this habit change.[2] By establishing a clear vision of a positive workplace culture—rather than a world defined by the fear of harassment or termination—we can more effectively change some of the core habits that lead to sexual harassment in the first place.

Viewing sexual harassment prevention through a skills lens also requires us to consider the conditions that make learning possible. When building a skill around uncomfortable conversation, we are primarily moving people from conscious incompetence to conscious competence. In other words, we are asking people to see something that they know makes them uncomfortable and consciously choose to speak up rather than stay silent. According to research around the four stages of competence,[3] this process requires practice in a supportive environment and the freedom to make mistakes.

One final note: A skills-based approach does not tackle systemic oppression and difference in identities directly, though it provides many opportunities to explore the role of power and privilege through its practical application. Oftentimes, focusing on inherent biases can actually perpetuate them.[4] Additionally, without skills around uncomfortable conversations, discussions of identity can quickly become polarizing and unproductive. By focusing on uncomfortable conversations, we are also building the muscles required to support conversations across all kinds of difference—and the systems that oppress others because of that difference.

CHAPTER SUMMARY

▶ Compliance trainings cover the definitions, relevant—and evolving—laws, organizational policies, and reporting guidelines related to sexual harassment and misconduct.

▶ Compliance is a critical place to start training on sexual harassment prevention and response, because it spells out the rules for the organization and the consequences of breaking them. By placing compliance in a larger framework, organizations can lay the groundwork for effective skills-based approaches to preventing and responding to sexual harassment.

▶ A skills-based approach to preventing and responding to sexual harassment consists of establishing rules and expectations, assessing conversation experience, teaching The Uncomfortable Conversation Framework, engaging in practice conversations, and forming new habits.

▶ A skills-based approach leverages what we already know about organizational change, habit formation, and teaching and applies it to workplace behavior and relationships.

CHAPTER 2

YOUR CONVERSATION EXPERIENCE AND WHY IT MATTERS

Most people enter into sexual harassment training with unrealistic or undefined expectations, and it's left up to the facilitator to address all of these in a single two-hour training session or workshop. These unrealistic expectations range from a "cure" for sexual harassment to a script for every possible situation to a complete dismantling of power structures across gender, race, and income.

Reasonable expectations matter when it comes to skills, too. While it might be reasonable to expect yourself to memorize a company's sexual harassment policy in two hours, it's not reasonable to expect yourself to acquire life skills such as healthy relationships, boundary-setting, or providing support to those impacted by sexual violence within that time frame.

Imagine entering a roomful of people who need to learn French in a two-hour training session. A quick survey would reveal who grew up in France, who took French in high school, and who has never heard a word of French in their life. A smart approach would consider how to leverage those with the most experience to support those with less experience. A group consisting of 100 percent native English speakers requires a different approach than a group with mixed experience. Furthermore, if the group consisted of 90 percent bilingual French-English speakers, you'd have a pretty good chance of teeing up the French speakers to help their friends learn French.

When it comes to training on healthy relationships and appropriate behavior at work, understanding the specific kinds of experience of the people in the room informs you on how to go about building skills individually and as a group.

CASE STUDY **SHOULDN'T THIS BE OBVIOUS?**

"Shouldn't this stuff be obvious to people?"

At a kickoff meeting for a training engagement, the CEO expressed his frustration that he had to explain—and keep explaining—sexual harassment policy to his employees. Though I didn't mean to, I laughed, and then explained that he probably had more experience understanding behavior, boundaries, and relationships than the average employee.

Fortunately, he trusted my perspective and embraced the idea of surveying his employees on their experiences with conversations about sexual harassment and misconduct. A few days before the training, we sent the survey around to employees. To his surprise, nearly 85 percent took the survey. While there were a few grumblings about the instrument not being scientific enough, most people reported that they enjoyed the opportunity to reflect on the types of conversations they hadn't considered as a part of their professional experience and expertise.

The survey revealed several important findings for this particular organization.

- 77 percent felt experienced at defining sexual harassment and its impact, but less than half had actually handled a disclosure in a work setting.

- 4 percent of respondents did not feel comfortable addressing other people's troubling words or behavior.

- 55 percent of employees had received fewer than five hours of lifetime training on sexual harassment prevention and response.

- 16 percent of employees reported fewer than five hours of lifetime conversation on the topic of sexual harassment and violence.

When we shared the results with the CEO, he was still disappointed, and rightly so, that the skills and experience to prevent and respond to sexual harassment are not yet commonplace. However, he was also able to approach his leadership role in company-wide training with less frustration and a better understanding of what he needed to do in order to create a corporate culture that was safe and respectful for all genders. Sharing the results with the team in advance of the training also helped set reasonable expectations for why and how we covered the topics at hand. People with a lot of experience felt more comfortable holding back, and people with less experience knew they probably weren't alone in asking questions or trying out new approaches in conversation.

THE CHALLENGES AND OPPORTUNITIES OF DIVERSE EXPERIENCE

Maybe some of your colleagues were rape crisis counselors in college and spent countless hours supporting and advocating on behalf of survivors. This is valuable experience, but it doesn't necessarily make them skilled at helping others learn how to understand or change behavior that isn't appropriate in the workplace.

Maybe some of your colleagues grew up in a family where these issues were literally never discussed, and they are terrified at the thought of now talking about "private" topics in the workplace. Maybe some have heard a lot of stories about sexual harassment or others haven't heard any. In any case, this experience informs what information they find most interesting, their questions, and the skills they bring to your workplace culture.

Entering into a group discussion without a shared awareness about the variation in experience inevitably leads to challenges. In the case of learning French, we would never yell at a beginning French student for using incorrect vocabulary or for inadvertently saying something offensive. In the case of navigating uncomfortable conversations about sexual harassment or violence, it's possible that someone is stating something unskillfully or awkwardly, and simply needs to hear their idea reflected back in a more skillful way, not to be shut down altogether. When we understand that practice conversations are designed to build skills, we are more open to tolerating mistakes and do-overs, and therefore learning.

That's why an experience assessment is both an important part of kicking off your individual exploration of uncomfortable conversations and a critical part of facilitating conversations with a group. The experience assessment offers an opportunity to reflect on your conversation experience across a number of areas.

- Conversations growing up in your family with the people who helped raise you

- Conversations with those younger than you (children, siblings, nieces/nephews, or people you mentor)

- Conversations with survivors across genders

- Formal training on a variety of sexual harassment and violence topics in high school, college, or the workplace

Whether your total lifetime conversations are fewer than five or more than five hundred, there is always more to learn. This survey is simply a chance to reflect on the ways that the topic of sexual harassment and violence has shown up in your life, and the types of conversations that come most naturally to you. When you start from a place of honest assessment, this knowledge can inform the conversations you have and give you insights into the reactions and responses of your peers and colleagues, whose experiences may be different from yours.

INTRODUCING THE CONVERSATION EXPERIENCE ASSESSMENT TO YOUR TEAM

To utilize this survey with your team, provide context for the survey in advance through an introductory email (see sample on next page). Some people in the workplace may feel shocked when a survey inquires about conversations with their parents and loved ones about something like sexual abuse or assault. By conducting this survey in advance of further conversations about sexual harassment or violence, you set the stage for integrating the personal and professional in some new ways and allow employees to speak up if that's too much for them.

Please note that survey data should be collected anonymously and shared in the aggregate. The purpose isn't to focus in on any one individual's experience, but to understand the range of experience across a team or organization.

The experience assessment helps put a single group discussion about harassment in context for all participants. When we recognize that most employees have limited formal training on sexual harassment prevention and response, we can let go of the idea that a single, mandated ninety-minute seminar on sexual harassment will be sufficient. We can stop trying to pack everything into a one-size-fits-all webinar, and begin a long-term approach to developing behavioral and relational skills that will not just prevent sexual harassment but also make our work environments more productive.

When we recognize the range of experience in talking about various aspects of sexual harassment and violence, we begin to see the need for and the value of some guiding principles in those conversations. After you answer that range for yourself and your team, The Uncomfortable Conversation Framework described in the next five chapters will provide those guiding principles and suggest where and how you can use them.

SAMPLE INTRODUCTION TO THE CONVERSATION EXPERIENCE ASSESSMENT

This survey is designed to measure experience and comfort level with a broad range of conversations that inform your ability to have meaningful and productive conversations about sexual harassment in the workplace.

Though future discussions will be focused on sexual harassment in the workplace, the skills, experience, and comfort and discomfort we bring to the topic of harassment at work may come from our personal lives and upbringing. Some people may have a lot of experience talking about sexual harassment and misconduct—perhaps they volunteered as a crisis counselor in college or have a friend or intimate partner who experienced abuse. Some people may have very little experience talking about these topics as a result of their upbringing or lack of exposure.

In any case, your candid responses, which will remain anonymous, will help ensure that our future group discussions are meaningful and productive. No question is required. This is an opportunity to learn and reflect before our next session together.

CONVERSATION EXPERIENCE ASSESSMENT

Part One: **Comfort Level**

Please reflect on how comfortable you are with the following topics related to sexual harassment and abuse, and the contexts in which you might have those conversations. People have different reasons for feeling uncomfortable—sometimes it's lack of experience or fear of the conversation going the wrong way. Circle the number that best describes your experience, with 1 being extremely uncomfortable and 7 being extremely comfortable.

Defining sexual harassment in the workplace

       1   2   3   4   5   6   7

Describing the impact of sexual harassment
to my peers

       1   2   3   4   5   6   7

Responding to a disclosure of sexual
harassment in the workplace

       1   2   3   4   5   6   7

Setting boundaries in a professional context

       1   2   3   4   5   6   7

Receiving feedback on my behavior

       1   2   3   4   5   6   7

Supporting a female survivor of sexual abuse or assault

       1   2   3   4   5   6   7

Supporting a non-female (male or transgender)
survivor of sexual abuse or assault

       1   2   3   4   5   6   7

Discussing my own attitudes and behaviors
that may make others uncomfortable in the
context of sexual harassment or misconduct

       1   2   3   4   5   6   7

Addressing someone else's troubling words or behavior
that may constitute sexual harassment or misconduct

          1   2   3   4   5   6   7

Discussing sexual harassment on social media

          1   2   3   4   5   6   7

Talking about ways to make my workplace
friendlier to people who experienced sexual
abuse or assault in the past

          1   2   3   4   5   6   7

Part Two: **Estimated Conversation Experience**

*For the questions below, please estimate the number of
conversations you have had on each topic. These are designed to
be estimates, not exact numbers, and are useful in establishing
ranges. If it's a handful, you can say 3. If it's too many to count,
you can just say 150 or 200.*

Number of conversations with a parent or older
family members (someone who helped raise you)
about consent, impact of sexual violence, sexual abuse
prevention, or advocacy

       _____

Number of conversations with your own children
or nieces/nephews about consent, impact of sexual
violence, sexual abuse prevention, or advocacy

       _____

Hours spent in formal classes or workshops on
sexual harassment prevention or response

       _____

Hours spent in formal classes or workshops
on consent

       _____

Hours spent in formal classes or workshops on bystander intervention or other intervention techniques   _____

Hours spent in formal classes or workshops on healthy relationships   _____

Hours spent in formal classes or workshops on implicit bias   _____

Hours spent in formal classes or workshops on conflict management, accountability, and/or feedback   _____

Number of supportive conversations with a female survivor of sexual abuse or assault (not harassment)   _____

Number of supportive conversations with a non-female survivor of sexual abuse or assault (not harassment)   _____

Number of women who have informally shared stories about sexual harassment with you   _____

Number of men or transgender individuals who have informally shared stories about sexual harassment with you   _____

Number of times you have responded in a managerial context to a disclosure of sexual harassment   _____

Number of conversations where you have addressed someone else's behavior or language that could be interpreted as sexual harassment or as offensive to survivors of sexual violence   _____

Number of times you have reported sexual
harassment to a manager or other formal
reporting mechanism   _____

Number of conversations where you have taken
accountability for your own behavior or language that
could be interpreted as sexual harassment or offensive
to survivors of sexual violence   _____

Number of times you have shared articles or
blog posts about sexual harassment or violence
on social media   _____

Other conversations about sexual harassment
or violence you've had in your life (list categories
and score):

_____   _____

_____   _____

_____   _____

_____   _____

_____   _____

_____   _____

TOTAL LIFETIME CONVERSATIONS   _____

_____

► *The conversation survey is also available through my website,*
  www.sarahbeaulieu.me. By using the online survey, you can
  compare your results to others who have completed it.

CHAPTER SUMMARY

▸ As with any skill-building work, it's critical to start with a baseline assessment of your skill and consider the range of skill that may exist on your team or in your organization.

▸ By using a simple survey, you can reflect on your own experience of engaging in conversations about sexual harassment prevention and response and how that experience may compare with the experience of others.

▸ If used as part of team or organizational assessment, the survey can provide insightful data on an organization's collective experience and awareness about sexual harassment and show where differences in experience might get in the way of productive conversations.

▸ Group survey data should always be collected anonymously and shared in the aggregate. Survey tools and guidance are available in this chapter or on my website, www.sarahbeaulieu.me.

THE UNCOMFORTABLE
CONVERSATION
FRAMEWORK

CHAPTER 3

KNOW THE FACTS

This chapter and the four chapters that follow describe the five-part framework for uncomfortable conversations. Before we get started with the first of those five, Know the Facts, let's take a deeper look at why the Framework is important.

WHY USE A FRAMEWORK?

I developed the Framework after a two-year listening tour designed to understand the obstacles to speaking about sexual violence and engaging in prevention work. I spoke to hundreds of leaders in the field of sexual violence prevention and response, organizations dedicated to working with survivors, and leaders from other sectors and industries in business, nonprofit, and government. At the time, there were shockingly few resources available for men on healthy relationships, boundaries, changing culture, or supporting people who have experienced sexual abuse or assault. To further my perspective and understanding, I held in-depth interviews with more than fifty men of varied ages and backgrounds and surveyed hundreds of others to gain insights into how they approached these topics and where they could use additional support. The Framework, and each element of it, reflects what I learned through this process.

The Framework is less of a step-by-step approach and more of a mindset, a set of guiding principles, that will build your capacity

**THE UNCOMFORTABLE
CONVERSATION
FRAMEWORK**

Know the Facts

Get Uncomfortable

Pause the Reaction

Embrace Practical Questions

See the Whole Picture

to engage in more meaningful and productive conversations about sexual harassment and violence, conversations that benefit our relationships and organizations. Before diving into practice conversations in more specific areas, such as helpful intervention, providing support to others, or navigating boundaries for behavior, you'll want to ground yourself in these five principles.

Using this Framework is important because it provides common expectations for a conversation, how it might feel, and what it might be able to accomplish. Without an established common framework, we bring other frameworks that may or may not serve the purpose of a meaningful and productive conversation. In the case of sexual harassment, we frequently bring right/wrong, winners/losers, and men/women as central frameworks. Polarizing frameworks such as these can prevent us from engaging in the necessary conversations that support healthy relationships and workplaces.

The Uncomfortable Conversation Framework is gender-inclusive. When men and women are pitted against each other in a workplace conversation about behavior, that prevents the ongoing dialogue necessary to actually change behavior and establish healthy relationships across genders. Messaging that projects that men are always wrong and women are always victimized is too simplistic. People of all genders contribute to a climate and culture of silence. By engaging in more productive and meaningful conversations, all of us are empowered to participate positively in creating and supporting a culture that is healthier for everyone.

When you and your colleagues understand the kinds of conversations you'll have about sexual harassment through the same framework, it becomes easier to make them productive and to keep them going, key elements of effective prevention. With this as background, let's get started with a discussion of Know the Facts, one of the five guiding principles of the Framework.

FACTS YOU MAY NOT KNOW

The topic of sexual harassment and violence has been taboo for so long that many of the issues are shrouded in myths and misperceptions. To have a productive uncomfortable conversation, it helps to know the facts. Many people wade into conversations about sexual harassment and misconduct with limited, or even incorrect, information.

Let me say up front that I am not talking about knowing the facts about a particular incident of sexual harassment, abuse, or assault, as you might need to know if you were a detective or investigative journalist. I'm talking about facts that contribute to our ability to engage in uncomfortable conversations—facts you know, facts you don't know, and facts that may be unknowable.

What facts do you need to know? You need to know that sexual harassment is prevalent. Since the #MeToo movement first sparked an increase in media coverage of sexual harassment in 2017, new facts about sexual harassment have continued to emerge. Depending on the industry or sector, rates of sexual harassment range from 25 to 85 percent.[1] While certain groups—those who work alone; those who work in male-dominated industries or organizations; immigrants or undocumented workers; or food and hotel service workers, for example—are more likely to experience sexual harassment, no industry is immune.[2] As the media and other researchers continue to survey industries and sectors about sexual harassment, it's important to stay informed about new data and trends as they emerge.

You need to know how frequently sexual harassment is reported. We know that a significant percentage of people—up to 75 percent—do not report incidents of sexual harassment to their employers.[3] There are lots of reasons for not reporting: fear of social or professional retaliation, fear of inaction, fear of action that is *too* severe, fear of not being believed.

Workplace sexual harassment doesn't take place in a vacuum. It's critical to consider the facts about other types of sexual violence. The prevalence and aftermath of sexual abuse and assault in the places we live, learn, and pray directly affect the kinds of conversations we have about sexual harassment in a workplace setting.

In the United States, more than one in three women experience sexual violence in their lifetimes.[4] So do one out of six men.[5] Among transgender or nonbinary individuals, rates of sexual violence are often significantly higher.[6] Sexual violence impacts all races and ethnicities, though Native Americans and multiracial populations are disproportionately affected by sexual violence of all forms.[7] If your organization employs individuals from other countries, it's possible that rates of sexual abuse, assault, and other forms of sexual violence are much higher, depending on the country. Survivors are among us every day, whether they have disclosed to us or not.

You need to know what we already know about sexual harassment and violence prevention. Deeper research across discrete types of organizations such as the military,[8] prisons,[9] and college campuses[10] has helped illuminate facts around obstacles to reporting, conditions that permit sexual violence to take place, and data about certain types of perpetrators. For example, campus research has shown the power of bystander intervention—speaking up at troubling behavior—as a strategy to reduce sexual harassment and violence, which is why Chapter 9 is dedicated to applying uncomfortable conversations in that context. A third-party evaluation of a bystander intervention approach called GreenDot found that a small number of trained bystanders resulted in statistically significant decreases in rates of sexual harassment and violence in both high school and college settings.[11]

You need to know that sexual abuse and assault can create lasting impacts on mental, emotional, and physical health. Survivors of sexual trauma can experience a multitude of short-term and long-term mental health challenges,[12] including alcohol and substance abuse, depression, and suicide. Victims of sexual abuse are more likely to drop out of school,[13] face homelessness,[14] and become involved with the juvenile justice system.[15] According to the Adverse Childhood Experience Study,[16] survivors also face higher rates of chronic health conditions, such as heart disease, diabetes, and obesity. Survivors who are able to access help and healing can overcome these challenges, but many face financial and social obstacles in finding effective treatment and support.

Organizations and society pay a heavy price for sexual harassment and other forms of sexual violence. A recent CDC study found that the lifetime financial burden of rape for a U.S. adult victim is more than $120,000.[17] These costs include lost work productivity, medical costs, criminal justice activities, and property damage or loss. When you consider this across the U.S. population, we're talking about more than $3 trillion. In Fiscal Year 2017, the U.S. Equal Employment Opportunity Commission collected $43 million on behalf of sexual harassment claims, which is just the tip of the iceberg in legal costs for companies, as most settlements are still held confidential.[18]

You need facts about perpetrators. A 2015 literature review, conducted by the RAND Corporation, found that perpetrators of sexual violence against women are driven by a combination of personal and environmental factors, including attitudes about sex, interpersonal skills, gender-related attitudes and cognitions, and perceptions of peer attitudes and behaviors.[19] Less is known about both male and female perpetrators against men.

Across the board, you need to know that gender is a part of this conversation, but it's not the whole conversation. Survivors exist across all genders. Perpetrators exist across all genders. All of us, regardless of gender, can contribute to a culture that allows harassment and violence to take place. All of us, regardless of gender, can support survivors as they heal. These are indisputable facts.

This isn't designed to be a chapter that will deliver all of the facts. The point is that facts can, and will, inform the kinds of conversations you have and how you have them. If these facts are new to you, consider the possibility that others already know them. If these facts are old news, consider the possibility that they may be new to someone else.

When entering into a conversation about sexual harassment and violence, ask yourself what you might not know that could be relevant to the conversation. You may need to take a break from a conversation to learn the facts or check out new information on your own. Ask yourself whether the person you are talking to has all of the facts, or may be misinformed. What is obvious to you may be in conflict with a belief that is deeply held by someone else, and cannot be overcome in a single conversation. Unless the facts—and our relationship to them—are on the table, we can't have a productive conversation.

STAYING OPEN TO FACTS

Sometimes, when confronted with apparently conflicting reports or statistics, we believe the "fact" that aligns with what we already believe. When we instead approach new information with a mindset that is open to it, we can dive below the surface and see more nuanced information that might change our perspective.

In 2018, the Equal Employment Opportunity Commission (EEOC), the leading federal agency in charge of handling complaints of sexual harassment, published a comprehensive report addressing workplace sexual harassment, including a review of existing surveys on this topic. Depending on the survey, the percentage of respondents reporting experiences of sexual harassment ranged from 25 to 85 percent.[20]

This is a wide range. Rather than ending their inquiry there, the authors of the report dug deeper into the facts that might explain the variation. What they learned provided valuable information to guide training, industry initiatives, and other next steps for the EEOC, organizations, and individual employees. The differences were primarily explained by the types of questions used to gather the data. Some surveys asked about sexual harassment more broadly, while others asked about specific behaviors that constitute sexual and gender-based harassment. When respondents were asked about specific behaviors, the resulting rates of sexual harassment were much higher. For example, employees might not consider sexual innuendo from customers to be sexual harassment, although it is legally defined as such, especially when experienced repeatedly.

This is an important takeaway that deepens knowledge and suggests future action and learning. For example, if managers are expected to report sexual harassment to human resources or handle reports in a particular way, it's critical that they fully understand which behaviors constitute sexual harassment. An employee may report a behavior but not call it sexual harassment.

While a range of data may, at first glance, cause confusion, the reality is that all research provides insights and evokes additional areas of learning. If the range is viewed as a conflict or a problem, we tend to focus on the problem rather than on what we can learn about how the range of data came to be.

The polarizing nature of public dialogue on this topic can make it challenging to interpret and understand the facts. In the example above, it's easy to imagine dramatic media headlines designed to provoke conflict—for example, *The Equal Employment Opportunity Commission Can't Agree on Rates of Sexual Harassment* or *Survey Design Leads to Inaccurate Data on Sexual Harassment.*

When presented with new facts on a taboo topic like sexual harassment or violence, you can apply a Know the Facts mindset to resist the urge to be pulled into a polarized, unproductive conversation by using the following tips:

- Read the actual report, not the headline about the report. The headline is supposed to make you click on the article, but doesn't always tell the whole story.

- There will always be ranges in data, especially when it comes to reporting on this topic. Learn how survey design or sampling approaches might explain different results.

- Surveys on incidences of sexual harassment and violence are tricky to design. For example, responses to a broad question about experiences of sexual harassment might yield different results than a series of questions about more specific behaviors or experiences. Read about the methodology and approach, and consider how it might affect the results.

- Some people simply don't believe any data. Don't let the online conspiracy theorists and skeptics spark doubt. The Internet today can give the same equal voice to opinion, extreme doubt, and personal narrative as it does to data and facts. Learn to tell the difference.

THE ROLE OF FACTS IN UNCOMFORTABLE CONVERSATIONS

Part of the Know the Facts mindset is discerning when a discussion or review of facts is or is not central to a particular conversation. While understanding the facts about sexual harassment and violence is a critical element of engaging effectively in conversations that will improve workplace culture, it's not reasonable to expect all of your colleagues to know all of the facts, all of the time. We've already seen how each of us has a diverse set of relationships and opportunities that have grounded our experience in talking about sexual harassment and violence. This means that you will frequently find yourself in a conversation with someone who doesn't know all the facts outlined in the first part of this chapter.

Sometimes the purpose of a conversation is to teach someone a new fact or set of facts. For example, if I were presenting the findings of the Conversation Experience Assessment to the executive team of an organization, we would talk about the survey, the questions, and the results. The entire purpose of the discussion would be to make sure the group understood the facts of the data and how to interpret them for future trainings.

In other cases, the purpose of the conversation is something else entirely. In those conversations, you may discover that someone might not be working from the same set of facts as you are. When this happens, it can be tempting to "correct" misinformation or set the record straight. However, there can be facts—or "alleged" facts—that aren't actually relevant to the conversation at hand.

For example, if you find someone unconscious on the street, you don't have to agree on the cause of the injury to agree that the person needs medical attention. In the same way, you don't need to agree that systemic oppression is the root cause of sexual violence to agree that it's important to treat colleagues reporting sexual harassment with empathy and respect. You don't need to agree on the intention of someone's words or behavior to agree that those words had an effect on someone else's sense of safety at work. This doesn't mean that you won't circle back and have a follow-up conversation about the facts—it's just a reminder to be intentional about using facts as tools to support a productive conversation versus using them as weapons that prevent productive conversations from unfolding.

The central questions to ask yourself when you come across a fact someone else may not know are:

- Is the fact relevant to this particular conversation?

- Is now the time to teach this person a new fact?

- Am I the right person to teach it?

It may take several conversations to help people learn new facts, or to learn them yourself. When we open ourselves up to conversations with the purpose of benefiting our relationships and workplaces, knowing the facts becomes a journey rather than a test. It's this kind of learning mindset that will lead to more productive and meaningful conversations.

CHAPTER SUMMARY

▶ The Uncomfortable Conversation Framework, developed through a focused listening tour and hundreds of interviews, reflects the key elements of a meaningful and productive conversation about sexual harassment and violence. The Framework recognizes that the topic of sexual harassment and violence evokes strong feelings and emotions and frequently falls into other less helpful and more polarizing frameworks.

▶ Starting with the facts creates opportunities to break through cultural myths and misperceptions that frequently show up in conversations about workplace sexual harassment. When it comes to sexual harassment and violence, many people do not know the basic facts about prevalence and impact, which are covered in this chapter.

▸ When we are presented with "new information" about sexual harassment and violence, we should be savvy about whether this information is being packaged to align with someone's existing beliefs—or whether it is actually new, credible, and useful information relevant to the discussion at hand.

▸ When we use facts as tools to support productive conversations, we can learn how to navigate conversations productively even when we don't agree on the same facts.

CHAPTER 4

GET UNCOMFORTABLE

THE INEVITABILITY OF DISCOMFORT

Every single time I train a new group of employees, I share a little bit about my personal experience with sexual abuse and assault. Usually it's just a few sentences mentioning that I'm personally a survivor, or I offer a quick anecdote, like the one about the first conversation with my mother (see the Preface). And, every single time, the same thing happens. My face gets hot. I start to sweat. I take off my jacket or sweater. My heart pounds in my chest. Thoughts rush through my head. I wonder whether people think more or less of me. I wonder whether they think I'm unstable or not really a professional. I wonder if I'm going to inadvertently trigger someone simply by saying the words.

No matter how many times I speak or share my story, I feel uncomfortable every single time I do it—both in my body and in my mind. The amount of experience I've amassed in my lifetime doesn't matter a bit. It's just an uncomfortable topic, and I'll always feel uncomfortable when I talk about it.

Whether you're sharing a personal experience, speaking up about someone's behavior that may or may not be inappropriate, or asking a clarifying question, talking about sexual harassment is uncomfortable. That's why Get Uncomfortable is the second element of The Uncomfortable Conversation Framework. Through

THE UNCOMFORTABLE CONVERSATION FRAMEWORK

Know the Facts

Get Uncomfortable

Pause the Reaction

Embrace Practical Questions

See the Whole Picture

my research and interviews, I've realized that discomfort is pretty much the name of the game whenever the topic of sexual harassment comes up. There are several reasons for this, which we'll dive into later in this chapter.

Let's consider running, another favorite sport, because this aligns well with uncomfortable conversations. If you've ever gone for a run, you know it's not the most comfortable exercise in the world. I don't consider myself a runner, but I do like to run. If I stopped running every time it felt uncomfortable, I wouldn't make it farther than the distance between the door of the supermarket and my car in the parking lot—in the pouring rain.

But I don't run to avoid discomfort. I run because my head clears after about twenty minutes. I run because it's the most effective and efficient form of cardiovascular exercise, and I want to be fit and healthy. Sometimes I also have to run because I'm trying to catch my small children before they dash into the street.

Discomfort isn't always a sign that we should avoid something. Sometimes the discomfort is just part of the process. When it comes to sexual harassment and violence, discomfort simply means we're having the conversation at all.

In my research and listening tour, I've dug deeper into the discomfort, and in doing so I have discovered that it comes from a wide range of understandable places. The first, and biggest, is that conversations about this topic require us to confront conflicting things that are true at the same time. In my own life, I will never be able to reconcile the fact that I loved the family members who molested me *and* they horrifically sexually abused children. In a workplace setting, it's likely that you will know—and possibly even like—both people involved with an inappropriate interaction while it's being investigated. Sitting with two conflicting truths at the same time is always uncomfortable. There's nothing that can make this go away.

Other aspects of this topic bring up discomfort in people. The mere thought of sexual abuse and assault requires us to face the reality that the people we love and trust can cause deep and irreparable harm to us. If you are a survivor of sexual abuse or assault, this feeling of being overwhelmed and helpless may be familiar—which doesn't make it any less uncomfortable. If you haven't experienced this kind of trauma or betrayal directly, the topic of sexual violence hammers home the fact that, at any given moment, our safety is uncertain. If you can't trust the people you love not to harm you, whom can you trust? How can you feel safe in the world? How can we protect ourselves from harm? We tend to focus on victims in these stories because if we can distance ourselves from the victim, we can maintain our illusion of safety and control. Yet if we avoid feeling uncomfortable in these conversations, we're also avoiding the victims, the reality of what those victims need to heal, and our complicity in the shame and silence that makes that healing difficult.

In terms of sexual harassment in a workplace context, it can feel uncomfortable to recognize that our perspectives on this topic are informed by experiences and conversations that took place outside of work. When our personal and professional worlds collide, we can no longer compartmentalize our emotions. For example, if you—or a close friend or partner—experienced harassment in another job, you may not want to share that information at your current job, even though it could be relevant to the discussion. Or, if you grew up in a family that never talked about healthy relationships or appropriate workplace behavior, that might not be something you want to mention to your boss—or to your subordinates. While we aren't required to share our personal selves at work, the lack of information about our colleagues' experiences outside of the workplace leaves us flying blind in conversations.

Finally, many of us struggle with finding the magic words that will make all of these problems go away. Sadly, there is no one "right" thing you can say to people who have experienced harassment or assault to heal them. There's no one command you can give to a potential perpetrator that is guaranteed to stop that person from hurting someone. The secret sauce is, in fact, the discomfort we are willing to make ourselves feel. It's uncomfortable, knowing that you are probably going to have to keep making yourself uncomfortable if we want a world free of harassment and violence.

That's the bad news. The good news is that, with practice, you can get better at tolerating the discomfort. The more you put yourself in the position of feeling uncomfortable, the better you get at recognizing the experience of discomfort in your body and mind. When you realize you can feel uncomfortable and still engage in conversation, the possibilities for that conversation open up in new ways. The other good news is that it's liberating to realize that everyone is uncomfortable, not just you. You aren't alone in your discomfort.

As you gain more experience with uncomfortable conversations and begin to apply them to specific skills in the workplace, discomfort manifests itself in a host of ways. Simply engaging in a conversation that someone else initiated can be quite uncomfortable for many people. For others, the discomfort particularly focuses on specific kinds of conversations: receiving feedback on behavior or setting boundaries or hearing about an incident of sexual harassment or assault. Most conversations that prevent and respond to sexual harassment require both parties to tolerate a level of discomfort that may be new for them.

HOW TO RESPOND TO DISCOMFORT

You don't need to know the source of discomfort—for yourself or someone else—to engage in a productive uncomfortable conversation. However, recognizing the source can better help you to work through it. When we run, we know the difference between feeling out of breath and a pebble in our shoe. Both are uncomfortable, but require different strategies to ease the discomfort while we continue our run. With uncomfortable conversations, the key to navigating discomfort is to bring it into the conversation transparently so we can address it and move on.

The following three-page chart, "Sources of Discomfort," provides examples of the kinds of uncomfortable thoughts that might arise during a conversation, a potential source of the discomfort, and how to bring that source into the conversation in a clear, nonjudgmental way.

This chart concludes the overview of Get Uncomfortable, the second part of The Uncomfortable Conversation Framework. Then we will move on to Chapter 5 and the third part of the framework, Pause the Reaction.

SOURCES OF DISCOMFORT

What You Might Think	Source of Discomfort	How to Name the Discomfort in Conversation
They clearly don't care about victims. How could they say something like that?	You identify strongly with a victim, and someone makes a comment about the perpetrator or the accountability process.	There's really nothing this person could have done to deserve to be treated this way AND I want to live in a world that treats the accused fairly and with dignity and respect.
Why are they bringing this up? I thought people were innocent until proven guilty.	You identify strongly with the perpetrator or believe an accountability process is unfair, and someone makes a comment about the impact on the victim.	There's really nothing this person could have done to deserve to be treated this way AND I want to live in a world that treats the accused fairly and with dignity and respect.
Did they not get my joke? They really need to lighten up.	You find a joke to be funny, and a few people tell you it offended them.	Oh, gosh. It wasn't my intention to offend you, but clearly I did. I'd love to hear more about why you found it offensive.
It just feels like we are talking over each other. This person doesn't get it.	You are confronted with an idea that conflicts with something true for you.	Maybe we are having two conversations? Both are probably important, but maybe not related to each other. It can be hard to unpack this topic.

Does that even happen?	You are confronted with an experience or perspective that doesn't make sense to you.	My truth/experience might be different from your truth/experience in this situation, but I'm willing to listen and learn more.
I want to say something, but I'm afraid I'll make the other person more upset.	You don't know the right thing to say to someone who has experienced sexual abuse or assault.	I'm here to support you, but am having trouble finding the right words. I'll keep trying, and hopefully you can let me know what helps the most.
Gosh, why are they asking me? What if I say the wrong thing?	You are asked for advice about how to respond to an incident of sexual harassment and don't know what to say.	There are lots of different ways to respond. It really depends on your particular circumstance and what you are looking for. Maybe we can start with that?
If they aren't going to do the right thing, that's their issue.	You are asked for advice about how to respond to an incident of sexual harassment, and it's not received well by the other person.	Maybe there's something I'm not fully understanding about your perspective. What's right for me might not be right for you.
I can't believe s/he would do that—they are such a GOOD person.	You have a relationship with someone who was accused of sexual harassment or misconduct.	It's hard knowing that someone we respect might intentionally or unintentionally cause harm to someone else.

Sources of Discomfort, cont.

What You Might Think	Source of Discomfort	How to Name the Discomfort in Conversation
It's just so horrible. How did this person survive this?	You are hearing about the impact of sexual abuse or assault for the first time.	It's painful to hear these stories, and I know how important it is for survivors to be heard.
This conversation is ridiculous. It's pointless.	You frequently speak up about harmful behavior and troubling attitudes, and haven't seen the changes you want to see.	Speaking up takes a lot of energy and effort. It's also a necessary tool to create change. I'm going to sit this conversation out.
This is NOT appropriate to talk about!	You never talked about bodies, boundaries, or sex in your family, religion, or culture.	These are things we never talked about in my family, religion, or culture, so I feel uncomfortable talking about them today.
Why aren't they saying anything?	You think someone else is uncomfortable.	Oh, I guess we are getting into uncomfortable territory.
Can this conversation just be over? I don't want to talk about this stuff anymore.	You are uncomfortable, but aren't sure why.	This conversation is making me feel (<u>emotion</u>). Can we come back to it later?

CHAPTER SUMMARY

▶ Conversations about sexual harassment and violence are inevitably uncomfortable. When we expect this to be the case, we don't stop or avoid talking about sexual harassment when the discomfort arises.

▶ While discomfort can come from many different places, learning to recognize the source of discomfort can help you move through it more effectively.

▶ Even as you gain experience in uncomfortable conversations, the discomfort—for all people engaged in a conversation—remains a constant.

CHAPTER 5

PAUSE THE REACTION

WHY TAKE A PAUSE?

We've all seen conversations about sexual harassment go south, and fast. One of the most important things we can do to invite meaningful conversations is to learn how to pause our own reactions—and the reactions of others—so we can continue the conversation long enough to find a moment of insight or understanding. You can't stop yourself—or others—from reacting, but you can take a moment before you respond. Learning how to pause will give you the mental space to validate your own feelings, but then to think through how you might want to approach the rest of the conversation.

HOW TO GET CURIOUS, NOT FURIOUS

Let me share an example of how pausing the reaction can contribute to more meaningful conversations. At a conference reception, I recently met four men from various tech companies across the country. I asked them one of my favorite icebreaker questions: "How has #MeToo changed the kinds of conversations you have at work?"

One of the men responded that he now restrains himself when telling jokes. "I no longer tell offensive jokes in front of women," he said, making it clear that he still tells them, just not in front of women.

**THE UNCOMFORTABLE
CONVERSATION
FRAMEWORK**

Know the Facts

Get Uncomfortable

Pause the Reaction

Embrace Practical Questions

See the Whole Picture

I paused, considering my next move. I knew nothing else about this young man, other than the statement he had just made. He wasn't making the best first impression, but I was curious to learn more. I was also curious about the others in the group. Instead of calling him out, I continued the conversation.

The other men in the group had very different responses. One of them said, "My wife and I talk more about how to raise our daughter with a better understanding of consent."

Another talked about his role as a leader, and how he struggled to figure out the right ways to address behavior he knew was troubling. Both of these men shared some of their surprise and sadness at how the culture was harmful to female colleagues.

During this conversation, I asked them all whether they had talked about this stuff growing up with their parents or in school. The guy who had made the comment about offensive jokes immediately responded that he hadn't even considered this topic until the #MeToo movement broke.

After speaking about my work in a little more depth, I turned back to him and said, "Hey, so I'm curious about the jokes. What makes them funny?"

"What do you mean?" he asked.

"Well, I mean just that. Like, my seven-year-old son likes to tell poop jokes. He thinks they're funny because people laugh when he tells them, but most people aren't laughing at the joke. They're laughing because this little kid is cracking himself up. So there are lots of reasons people tell jokes and laugh at them, right? Jokes being funny is only one possible reason."

I turned to the other guys and asked, "Do you ever laugh at jokes you don't think are funny?"

All three said yes.

The first guy frowned. "So maybe the fact that I think these jokes are funny is a problem?"

"Maybe," I said. "Maybe the jokes aren't as funny as you think they are. Or maybe they aren't funny to as many people as you think they are."

Now, I could have eye-rolled at his first comment and called him out, but I didn't. My intention in the conversation was to learn and to influence, not to lecture. My intention wasn't to shame or humiliate, just to better understand a perspective that wasn't mine.

By pausing my own reaction, I found a way to engage in the conversation productively. I know that a single conversation with a stranger at a conference won't permanently change one person's lifelong perspective on gender and prevent them from ever telling another offensive joke. But I also know that calling someone out harshly—a common response to statements like this—would have shut the entire conversation down, including the discussion with the other men. The young jokester had an opportunity to hear how managers and leaders felt about offensive jokes. We kept it going and all learned more about each other and our perspectives. In fact, one of the men in this group walked away inspired enough by our discussion to have thirty conversations about sexual harassment in thirty days—an opportunity that never would have come up if I had shut down the conversation at the beginning.

My mantra in most conversations is "Get curious, not furious." It's actually a phrase I picked up in a parenting class, but it nicely summarizes the practice and purpose of this part of The Uncomfortable Conversation Framework. Following are three practical suggestions for applying this phrase in a conversation.

▶ TO THOSE WHO ARE UNDERSTANDABLY ANGRY

Please understand that I'm not saying you can't be angry, or that there is something wrong with anger. And I'm not talking about reactions to being personally harassed or assaulted. Sometimes a strong reaction, especially anger, is what the situation calls for, and rightly so. Anger, when expressed in healthy ways, is an important element of relationships, organizations, and movements.

Sometimes people are angry at the direct experience of injustice, or they are tired of witnessing persistent, systemic bad behavior that seems intractable and hopeless. I hear this comment quite frequently, especially from women who have experienced frequent or persistent sexual harassment. You have a right to be mad. You are within your rights to express your anger. Expressing anger can be a way to reclaim your power. My point isn't that anger is wrong or unnecessary. It's that anger alone isn't going to solve the problem.

Imagine this. A woman walks down the street past a group of men. The men catcall the woman, making vulgar comments about her body and how they want to have sex with her. She turns around, screams at them in anger, and walks away. Her anger provided a moment to reclaim her power and ultimately reduce the impact or trauma of the vulgarity.

Furthermore, her anger expressed, in no uncertain terms, that this behavior was unacceptable. We should absolutely be angry when people treat us without dignity and respect. Anger breaks things open and brings injustice or bad behavior to the surface.

However, in order for behavior to change, these men are going to need someone to help them understand the effect of their behavior and teach them new skills. Anger might create a motivation to change, but no one can learn from an angry teacher. When we confuse anger with teaching, we will be disappointed with the results.

In workplace conversations about sexual harassment, people who have experienced repeated harassment may be justifiably angry. When this anger is expressed in the workplace, it may feel outsized to the incident at hand when, in reality, it's the accumulation of incidents that haven't yet been addressed. It's reasonable to be angry at injustice. A person who feels angry in a conversation or discussion is bringing something important to the table. Sometimes it's important not to pause an angry reaction, because it helps others really understand the impact of their action or inaction.

If someone says something that angers you, be angry. But to the extent possible, given the circumstance, use your anger in intentional ways and directions.

- At the first sign of irritation, annoyance, or anger, take a pause. Breathe. Remember why you are engaging in the conversation in the first place.

- Assume good intent. Unless a comment is abusive or threatening your safety, consider inviting at least one more exchange.

- Be intentional in your response. In some cases, showing anger or annoyance is exactly the right move—the pause gives you control in how you express it.

Remember, it's a lot easier to get furious *after* you've been curious, rather than the other way around.

Another way to think about this process is to imagine that you are speaking to someone across a language barrier. Let's say you're a native English speaker and a colleague from your Asia office is visiting. If he says something you don't quite understand, or misuses an English phrase in a way that translates to something offensive, your first reaction probably wouldn't be to berate him. Yelling at people doesn't teach them English. When it comes to behavior, relationships, and workplace interactions, we're all learning a new language, putting together awkward sentences, trying out words for the first time and learning while we're doing it.

When we pause our own reactions, we can learn more about others' reactions and perspectives. Over time, pausing gives us more time to learn the tools we need to advance the way we understand and interact with each other.

BIG REACTIONS, BIG PAUSES

One of my early forays into talking about sexual violence publicly did *not* go very well. Back in 2012, I was still operating under the incorrect assumption that most men didn't want to talk about sexual assault because they were afraid of being called rapists. Their silence, I concluded, must be defensiveness.

So I made a nice, pretty little graphic.[1] It compares the likelihood of being falsely accused of sexual assault with the likelihood of going to jail if you actually rape someone. In my mind, at the time, this was a lighthearted way of pointing out that men are more likely to get away with rape than to be falsely accused. To a non-rapist, this should be great news, right?

Wrong. I posted the graphic on Tumblr one January evening and went to bed. It was my third post on Tumblr—ever. When I woke up, the graphic had been shared 16,000 times. I picked up the phone and called my brother, who knew more about Tumblr than I did. He informed me this was not the normal course of things online.

The number of shares continued to tick up, and up, and up—and then the media caught wind of it. By the end of the next day, I had learned several important lessons.

LESSON #1. If Dylan Matthews from the *Washington Post*[2] publishes your graphic, the rest of the world assumes you are a data scientist. I am not. My approach was logical, but not scientific.

LESSON #2. The explanation of a graphic doesn't go viral with the image, and 90 percent of people comment without fully understanding what they are commenting on. (See Chapter 3, "Know the Facts.")

LESSON #3. False accusation is the third rail of sexual violence conversations.

The Internet exploded. Overnight, I was equally critiqued by some of the top feminist bloggers and the biggest men's rights activist threads on Reddit. To date, the graphic has been shared close to a million times, sparking a whole host of unproductive conversations about sexual violence. Here is a sampling of blog post titles and headlines:

- This Rape Infographic is Going Viral. Too Bad It's Wrong[3]

- Rape Statistics. The Anatomy of a Lie[4]

- Show this Depressing Graphic to the Rape Apologist in Your Life[5]

Online commentators were really angry, for all sorts of reasons. I was called a feminist—in positive and negative ways. I was called a liar, a manipulator, an advocate, a crazy woman. Some people saw the graphic as proof that women never lie about sexual assault. Some saw it as proof that women use statistics to create rape hysteria. It seemed like every stranger had a different opinion about who I was, why I had made this graphic, and what it meant. And the worst part: The graphic wasn't being used to start or deepen a productive conversation. It was being used to prove a point and shut further conversation down.

If you've ever been on the receiving end of a viral backlash to an online post or comment, take the expert advice: don't read the comments. Of course, I didn't take the expert advice. I read the comments—hiding in my bed, of course, as my husband tried to wrestle the phone out of my hand. It was a dark couple of days. I felt simultaneously sad, overwhelmed, angry, and confused.

At first, I didn't engage. I gave myself time to calm down. And then I began to experiment with ways of responding to the comments. I did some more blog posts and responded directly to comments. I also reached out to reporters and bloggers directly and reflected on what I was hearing and learning. In some cases, the conversations didn't go anywhere—the other people either dug deeper into their reactions or took my response as a reason to further attack me. But in many cases, the initial reactions gave way to much more meaningful conversations, and these helped me gain insights into myself and into the strong reactions to the graphic.

On the one hand, the reactions were feedback on the way I had started the conversation with a particularly charged topic—false accusation of rape. I took the feedback to heart, and it led me to the series of interviews I conducted with men to more deeply understand male perspectives on sexual violence. On the other hand, the reactions were not always about me at all. I learned that the concept of a victim not being believed *and* the concept of an innocent person being accused of—or punished for—a crime they didn't commit touched on taboo topics that were not frequently discussed. The reaction was a sign of having a lot to say and feel, and not all the words to express it. The unpracticed conversations were there all along, but when I triggered them, the blowback came to me personally.

In an issue as taboo and under-discussed as sexual harassment and violence, we will frequently encounter unpracticed conversations bursting with emotion, whether the conversations take place at home, at work, or online. The emotional reactions vary from person to person and from conversation to conversation. That's often the point.

THE BLAME GAME

Reactions come from lots of different places. When we receive feedback on our behavior, hear comments or jokes we find offensive, or don't have our perspectives immediately understood or validated, we often react without considering the context.

Perhaps someone is reacting to the behavior because of a misconception or falsehoods that person learned from a trusted family member or friend. Perhaps someone else is frustrated after having to frequently explain the same concept over and over again. Or maybe someone is a survivor and has never told anyone, or that person is coming to terms with the reality that their past actions may have caused people to be scared.

One reaction we commonly experience in conversations about sexual violence and harassment is blame. Blame is a particular type of anger focused on making another person or group feel small or insignificant. I'm going to suggest pausing blame just as I suggested pausing anger. But before I do that, I want to be totally clear that I am not suggesting that we overlook bad behavior or ignore it. People who violate policies or commit crimes must be held accountable and suffer the consequences. But indulging in a broad blame game can be counterproductive.

When it comes to sexual harassment and violence, we blame victims for making a big deal out of nothing. We blame perpetrators as irredeemable monsters. We blame victims for what they wear, their prior behavior, or other things that have nothing to do with the incident at hand. We blame the people who report incidents for ruining the lives of those who are accused or we suspect their stories are not true. We blame people who don't report incidents by calling them cowardly or thinking they have something to hide. We argue about who deserves the most empathy, whose experience is the worst, which behavior is the most harmful. The next thing we know, we're pointing fingers at who is pointing fingers. We're yelling just to be louder than the yelling around us.

On the surface, the blame game is tempting. I have sometimes wished it had been a stranger who raped me. It's so much easier to blame a stranger. But the people who violated me—members of my family and, later, a male friend in high school—were people I loved, trusted, and welcomed into my life. Blaming them meant blaming myself for letting them close. The more I looked for someone to blame, the worse I felt about myself.

But here's something else I learned about blame. Blame distances us from each other. Blame makes us focus on the cause of the problem, not on how we might help create the solution. Blame doesn't call others or ourselves to a place of accountability and

▶ A PAUSE FOR MALE SURVIVORS

Knowing what I know about the prevalence of surviving sexual abuse or assault, the shame and stigma associated with those experiences, and the degree to which men lean into reactions that may look like anger, I will always pause my reaction and get curious in conversations with men. I'd rather respond with compassion to a man who holds troubling, or even abusive, attitudes than further alienate a man who can't find the words or emotions to express a traumatic past.

A quick story to illustrate this: When I worked as a rape crisis counselor, I was frequently called to meet survivors at the hospital to provide support and advocacy through a rape examination. On one shift, I was called to meet a survivor who had been accompanied to the hospital by a male friend. When I arrived, the staff briefing me on the situation told me that the male friend had been behaving in a disruptive way by challenging the nurses, speaking violently about the perpetrator, and so on.

Once I connected with the survivor, there was a moment

where she wanted some time alone to rest. I invited her friend to come help me find some snacks. As we walked through the hospital, we debriefed on how this experience had been for him, and normalized how traumatic it can be to see a friend in crisis. As it turned out, he was agitated for a reason. Witnessing his friend's response to being raped had triggered memories of his own sexual assault years before, and he was in the middle of a strong emotional reaction. The impact of sexual abuse and assault on men is made worse by our collective inability to see through men's reactions to the pain beneath. Even though this isn't a work story, I think about this man in almost every conversation I have about sexual violence at conferences or at company training sessions, because I know there are probably many men in the audience who won't come forward to share their own personal stories of sexual assault or abuse. I know and respect how much our personal histories affect how we relate to these issues on the job in our professional roles. I'd much rather give a man a little space to explain an angry or defensive reaction than shut down someone who experienced sexual violence and already feels alone.

restitution. Blame doesn't start a conversation. It ends one. And blame creates shame, which is what makes sexual violence so insidious in the first place.

In speaking with men about sexual harassment and violence, I've also learned that anger and defensiveness are common first reactions from men—and not because men are necessarily angry or defensive. Society teaches men not to be vulnerable or to express shame, sadness, or "softer" emotions. In professional settings, this pressure to be invincible can manifest itself across genders. Defensiveness is just that—a reaction in defense of a deeper vulnerability or feeling. For others, the initial reaction to a conversation about sexual harassment or violence might be tears. Crying may indicate sadness, trauma, overwhelm, shame, or even rage. When we react to people's reactions, the conversation gets off track, and we miss the opportunity to get any more information about what caused the reaction in the first place. When we can pause our reaction, we can continue conversations in more meaningful ways.

Now, we'll move on to the next element of The Uncomfortable Conversation Framework and learn how to apply curiosity in a conversation through Embracing Practical Questions.

CHAPTER SUMMARY

▸ When we expect and have a strategy for handling our own and others' reactions, we're more likely to work through challenges or differences in productive ways.

▸ Pausing a reaction of blame can be particularly challenging, because it's natural to seek out "right" and "wrong" around sexual harassment and violence. When we stop the blame game, we also stop the shame that contributes to unhealthy cultures and communities.

▸ Some people are understandably and justifiably angry. When faced with repeated injustice, anger is an appropriate and helpful response that can inform uncomfortable conversations.

▸ Men who react to conversations about sexual harassment with anger or defensiveness may simply be having a reaction related to surviving sexual abuse or assault themselves. When we pause our reaction, we can provide these survivors with a much-needed moment of empathy and connection.

CHAPTER 6

EMBRACE PRACTICAL QUESTIONS

WHAT IS A PRACTICAL QUESTION?

A practical question, in the context of The Uncomfortable Conversation Framework, is a question that illuminates the pathway toward healthier relationships and safer workplaces. It's a question grounded in genuine curiosity and asked from a place of a paused reaction. The purpose of a practical question is to learn, understand, and support deeper and more meaningful conversations. Practical questions help us make sense of where we might be missing each other in a conversation or where we might be speaking from different places of knowledge, experience, or sources of discomfort.

When a question is judgmental or asked out of a desire to shame someone, it doesn't advance a conversation—it shuts it down. There's so much we don't understand about each other's experiences, backgrounds, and perspectives that inform the way we behave and expect others to behave in the workplace. Oftentimes, our surface reactions and responses don't tell the whole story about who we are, how we feel, and what we believe.

A practical question, grounded in a pause, can help you figure out where the conversation might go next. In the case of the young man's comment about how he's telling offensive jokes only to men as a response to the #MeToo movement, a practical question gave

**THE UNCOMFORTABLE
CONVERSATION
FRAMEWORK**

Know the Facts

Get Uncomfortable

Pause the Reaction

Embrace Practical Questions

See the Whole Picture

him—and others—a chance to talk about humor, peer pressure, and why we tell offensive jokes. At other times, I've used practical questions to clarify what a person was actually saying, why they were saying it, what they really believe, and what they had been taught and by whom. When you encounter a new perspective, even a potentially offensive one, you can say, "Tell me more about why you believe that to be true," or "That's a new perspective to me. Can you share a little more about it?"

Practical questions also play a role in creating a world that is more supportive of those who have experienced sexual abuse and assault. In the case of my own experience as a survivor, I learned that practical questions and conversations about survivor experience and the kind of support that was meaningful to me helped my friends show up for me—and for others in their lives—in stronger ways. My best friend in college, Russ, like most men, was taught to fight, flight, or fix—yet none of those responses seemed quite right in the moments when my trauma exploded in ugly ways. His heart knew how to feel, but he had absolutely no idea what to say. And, like most of us who want to support a survivor of sexual violence, Russ wanted to support me. He just didn't know how. Over time, Russ learned, through practical questions he asked both me and my therapist, that emotions—especially in the face of traumatic experiences—were perfectly normal. He couldn't make the feelings go away, but he didn't fear that the feelings were his fault or his responsibility to fix.

A few years into our friendship, I was having a particularly bad night, and ended up crawling into the back of my closet to cry. My three female roommates didn't know what to do, so they called

Russ, who came over right away. Russ opened the door to the closet, asked me if I needed anything, and handed me a box of tissues. He then took out his homework and sat on the floor outside my closet. Eventually, I stopped crying, came out, and asked for a hug. Practical questions make us more confident in our responses, and over time change the way we understand complicated issues like healing, relationships, and healthy boundaries.

THE ART OF ASKING

At the end of many of my workshops on sexual harassment, someone will ask about hugs or some other form of touch. It's usually in the form of a semi-sarcastic question about whether hugging is now an offense worthy of termination, or whether they will get fired if they casually touch someone in the workplace.

Typically, someone in the room will immediately jump in with one of two responses, neither of which is particularly helpful:

RESPONSE #1

Why would you ever think it was okay to hug someone in the workplace? No hugs. No touching. Nothing. Keep your hands to yourself. It's just not worth the risk.

RESPONSE #2

How could you even ask such an ignorant question? You must also think that men and women can't meet behind closed doors, don't you? You can't possibly think like that and advance gender equity in the workplace.

It's natural to want to provide a definitive answer to a question. It's also natural to infer a worldview or perspective based on very little information. But these instincts don't achieve the broader goal of creating a culture of safety and respect. Both responses dismiss the question and judge or even shame the person who asked it. Both responses drive toward a right answer that is the same for every person who asks the question. Neither one advances the group's understanding of what makes a hug appropriate or inappropriate, because they shut down the conversation.

This is a prime example of how practical questions come into play, especially if you can pause a reaction you may have to the tone of the initial question. Here is a handful of questions you might ask to get more practical:

- Are you always the person initiating the hugs?

- How often are the huggers bigger than you? How well do you know the hugger?

- What kind of hug is it? A side hug? A full body hug? A pat on the back? Does the hug last for more than ten seconds? More than sixty seconds?

- Does the person you are hugging *want* a hug? How do you know?

- Does the person you are hugging like hugs? From you? Always or sometimes?

- Have you talked about hugging with this person before?

- How do you respond if the person doesn't want a hug?

In conversations about sexual harassment and violence, we aren't always going to find correct, one-size-fits-all answers. That's one aspect of this topic that makes it so uncomfortable. Practical questions enable us to unpack hidden tensions, myths, and misperceptions in ways that keep the conversation going. A hug, in and of itself, is not a problem. Hugs are a way to show affection, empathy, and support. Giving and receiving hugs can be a good thing, even at work. The issue is that we don't always know if our hugs are welcome, or whether we're imposing an unwanted hug on someone who fears our size or power. On the one hand, we don't want one group of employees to always have to turn down hugs and face consequences for doing so. On the other hand, we don't want to give people hugs if they prefer fist bumps or high-fives.

Without discussing the topic of hugging, we miss the opportunity to explore these deeper concepts and really think them through. Through the questions, we imagine a future world and ourselves in it. Even more important, answering questions with more questions offers a chance to get to the core issue without a lecture.

When faced with the conversational challenge of providing support to a survivor, calling out an offensive or troubling comment, or checking in on someone's safety, most people aren't looking for a theoretical breakdown or oral history of how we have arrived at this moment. They aren't seeking to understand gender, power, privilege, or any other social construct that may have led to the conversation in front of them.

No, they want a script. They want to know which words should come out of their mouths next. It's unrealistic, unfortunately, to provide a script for every single possible scenario that could unfold in a person's lifetime. That's why we need to embrace and encourage practical questions, no matter how basic they are.

Practical questions are a form of practice, and it takes practice to improve our relationships and behavior in the workplace. Practical questions reflect our understanding of gender, relationships, power, and boundaries. By engaging with practical questions, we're directing the conversation into an area of skill, learning, or mutual understanding.

Practical questions can indicate that people are reflecting on a past experience through a new lens. This is a good thing, as it means that our past doesn't have to define our future. Practical questions mean people are practicing. Asking a practical question about a conversation or scenario in advance is better than fumbling in the moment. Go ahead and ask. These questions aren't embarrassing. They are real, and don't deserve judgment. Even if there isn't one right answer, the question opens up the conversation in all the right ways.

WHAT IF I GET CALLED OUT?

Sometimes people avoid practical questions because they are afraid someone will call them out for doing it wrong. For example, a male manager compliments a colleague's outfit and says she looks like she's ready for a date. Another woman overhears and reprimands the manager for what he said. The male manager asks what kind of compliments are appropriate these days, and both women get really upset.

Any type of feedback conversation can evoke shame and defensiveness. Sometimes a callout is the result of frustration and unspoken feedback that accumulates over a long period of time. In other cases, your question might be the straw that broke the camel's back. Sometimes people call out others as a way of offering feedback on the impact of words, behavior, or attitudes, or to introduce facts in a caring and compassionate way. At other times, someone may use callouts to shut down the conversation or shame another person.

Even if you are called out in a harsh way, it's not the end of the world. First, we all say and do things that hurt people, intentionally and unintentionally. Only you will have insight into your own intentions. Second, we can't learn unless we ask questions. If you have questions about appropriate behavior, relationships, or power dynamics, by all means, ask them. Third, you can respect the person's reaction while holding onto your right to ask the question. We can be unapologetic about our words or behavior while still feeling empathy for someone who was hurt by them. Likewise, we can regret what we say or do without agreeing with someone's conclusion about what that means about us as a person. Finally, we can't control whether or not people call us out. But we can control how we react to it. If your question is met with a callout, here are a few tips:

- Acknowledge the other person's reaction. For example, you might say, "Thanks for sharing that feedback with me. You've given me something to think about."

- Get curious about why your question set off a reaction. By practicing curiosity in the moment, you can reduce the risk of falling into a blame game.

- Maybe this isn't the right person or situation for your question. Consider whether there might be someone better equipped or experienced to help respond to it.

- Take some space and sort it out with someone you trust. Shame feeds on silence. If you feel ashamed about getting called out, the best antidote is a conversation about it.

- If you realize that your question came out wrong, take accountability for it. For example, "Yikes, my foot isn't tasting very good right now." Or "Wow, that really came out wrong. Can I try again?"

A callout may hurt in the moment, but it's not a reason to avoid uncomfortable conversations or to avoid asking your practical questions.

Next, we'll move on to the fifth and final element of The Uncomfortable Conversation Framework: See the Whole Picture. We'll see how pausing our reactions and embracing practical questions opens up the possibility of seeing conversations through a new, broader perspective. Then we'll wrap up Part II with an illustration of how the Framework plays out in conversations.

CHAPTER SUMMARY

▸ Practical questions are a tool to unpack conversations in a curious, nonjudgmental way.

▸ Practical questions can help you develop a deeper understanding of complex issues, ranging from supporting people who have experienced sexual abuse or assault to managing boundaries or behavior in the workplace.

▸ If someone responds to your question negatively, it's a chance for you to practice pausing your own reaction to assess what happened—it doesn't necessarily mean the question was the wrong question.

CHAPTER 7

SEE THE WHOLE PICTURE

THE WHOLE INCIDENT PICTURE

One thing that gets in the way of our ability to engage in a broad range of uncomfortable conversations is our tendency to narrow our view to one moment in time, one person, or one perspective. When we do this, we miss out on the opportunity to engage in the kinds of uncomfortable conversations that enable us to prevent incidents from taking place. Recently, I heard a story about a newly promoted manager who went to a junior colleague's room with a group of peers after a conference reception at their hotel. After a nightcap, the manager's peers left, but the manager was so intoxicated that he passed out on the couch. What happened next is unclear. The junior colleague said he tried to come into her bed in the dark, where she had fallen asleep after the others had left. The manager said he stumbled about and eventually returned to his own room. After some discussion and contemplation, the junior colleague reported it to human resources a few weeks later.

When sharing a story like this with others, I'll frequently hear some of the following questions or statements:

- Well, how do we know she's/he's telling the truth about what happened?

- What did she expect by hosting a party in her hotel room?

- If it was so wrong, why didn't she report it right away?

- Firing him is insufficient punishment. He should never be able to work again.

- He had a lapse in judgment. It shouldn't ruin his career permanently.

Comments like these illustrate how focusing on incidents outside of our personal experience tends to lead us down unproductive pathways, resulting in volatile, polarizing conversations. We focus on the incident, rather than seeing the context within which an incident took place.

Instead, we need to remember that multiple conversations may be necessary to achieve healthy relationships and safe workplaces. With that in mind, it becomes possible to imagine two sets of conversations emerging alongside each other, rather than in opposition. First, there is a set of conversations that will fully acknowledge the effect of this incident on the female colleague who felt scared. Even if the manager did not intend to scare the junior employee, he did. Second, there is a set of conversations that will help the manager understand his actions and how to take accountability for them. When we approach accountability conversations with empathy, rather than shame or humiliation, the entire organization or community benefits—even if the manager is ultimately terminated from his role. Empathy isn't in opposition to accountability—it's a critical part of it.

When we get stuck taking sides with either a victim or a perpetrator, we miss out on the chance to have meaningful conversations about accountability, rehabilitation, and redemption—characteristics of society and culture that are beneficial for all of us. Accountability is critical, even up to and including termination. Accountability is different from permanent shaming, permanent unemployment, or social ostracizing. These responses don't contribute to a culture that promotes safety and respect and don't reflect an understanding that most, if not all, human beings can grow and change through a combination of individual effort, coaching, and community support.

This dynamic plays out even more severely when it comes to sexual assault and rape. If we insist upon locking up any type of sexual offender and throwing away the key, we're expressing a belief that they are all the same and they cannot be rehabilitated. This belief factually isn't true, given what we know about different types of perpetrators, their motivations, and trajectories,[1] and it contradicts how we, as a society, respond to other kinds of crimes and criminals. It's possible to hold someone accountable for a crime like rape and to do so in a humane way.

When we separate conversations about people who commit harassment from conversations about the people who experience it, we can begin to understand the stories of how people become perpetrators or potential perpetrators and the role we all play in their evolution. Those stories are an important key to prevention. In this case, the young manager never considered that his colleagues might feel scared of him because of his gender and newfound power within the organization. Had he—or his managers—considered this an area of professional development, the entire situation could have been avoided in the first place.

When viewed through this lens we can understand and appreciate that a person who commits harassment will have friends and family who might not love their behavior, but will love them and their potential to change. As outsiders, we certainly don't have to personally love the perpetrator as their friends and family do, but we don't have to judge those who might be supportive of the perpetrator.

We can learn even more if we continue to broaden our perspective to include the whole picture, such as the spectrum of people who might have influenced the incident that night in the hotel room. Most immediately, where were his friends? Why didn't they take him safely back to his own hotel room? What about his boss? Did his company provide training that explored boundaries around managers socializing with subordinates? Did the career center at the manager's college teach him about sexual harassment and appropriate boundaries? What about the manager's high school teachers and coaches? Did they teach him about consent and boundaries? Did the high school superintendent provide funding to schools for teacher training on sexual harassment and violence prevention? Did parents demand it? Was sexual harassment prevention part of the citywide education agenda for the mayor in the manager's hometown?

The bottom line is that, when sexual harassment takes place, we are all responsible. Of course the person who perpetrates the assault shoulders a particular kind of accountability. However, our repeated, consistent inability to see beyond an incident in isolation means we're failing to prevent more incidents from taking place.

When we're participating in an uncomfortable conversation, it can be challenging to see it from a perspective that isn't our own. It's easy to get stuck in one place, or in one person's point of view. When that happens, we limit the kinds of conversations we can have in the moment, and the degree to which our conversations can impact the world around us. We can have many conversations that help us prevent and respond to sexual harassment and violence, and, in fact, the point is to make such conversations a practice and a habit.

THE WHOLE GENDER PICTURE

Learning how to see the whole picture can also mean learning to see how the same incident might be influenced by the genders and cultural backgrounds of the people involved. As I mentioned in the story about the male survivor who accompanied his friend to the hospital for a rape exam, he wasn't expressing frustration at his friend, but he was feeling triggered by her experience. In the case of the sales manager who couldn't understand why his colleague wouldn't go on sales calls with him, the truth is that he probably did do or say something that triggered fear or self-consciousness in his female junior.

The #MeToo movement has made it clear that many women feel afraid when they go to work. The fears women have are real and justified, grounded in a world that has consistently allowed harassment—and violence—to take place. Women's fear of sexual harassment—and of retaliation against reporting it—is commonplace, and is only now being discussed and addressed in more substantive ways.

But these fears aren't the whole picture. First, given the vast number of men and others who have experienced sexual abuse and assault, the fear doesn't belong to women alone. Second, the fear experienced by women—or victims—isn't the only dynamic at play. To see the whole gender picture, we also need to consider what it's like to be feared and rejected simply because of your gender.

As a woman, especially a white woman, I can go up to anyone on a train platform, ask them for the time, and expect a polite response. As a woman, I can lay my head down in a friend's lap and have a good cry. As a feminine woman in a heterosexual marriage, I can give and receive affection with other women without it being sexualized.

For a man, as I've learned, it's different. Being a man is akin to walking through life with a ferocious tiger by your side. The tiger is made up of a lifetime's worth of bad experiences other people may have had with male aggression and violence. People respond to the tiger, and usually don't take a moment to see very much about you. You may not personally be violent, but those around you act as if you could be at any moment. This takes a personal, emotional toll on how men walk through the world.

In some cases, men don't know the tiger is there. Since the tiger is invisible to them, these men can't understand why people respond to them with fear or defensiveness, so they become defensive in return. It is equally important for men and women to recognize this dynamic; men need to understand that the tiger is there and why, and women need to understand that men are often unaware of its existence. When we are able to see conversations about fear and conversations about being feared as aligned and not in opposition to each other, we can gain deeper understanding across genders.

When we consider the whole picture of gender, we see that people of all genders face similar struggles to be understood for who they are, and not just for what their gender represents. This perspective leads us to much more productive conversations about sexual harassment and violence.

THE WHOLE SURVIVOR PICTURE

The whole picture also impacts uncomfortable conversations through the experience of your colleagues who come to work already having experienced sexual abuse or assault.

Imagine this. Your mom dies.

You wake up the next morning, and no one is talking about moms or about death. You begin to question your reality. Am I the only one who has a mom who died? Maybe other people aren't as upset about their mom's death as I am. Whom do I talk to about this grief? Why isn't anyone asking about my mom?

Alternatively, you wake up the next morning to a thousand news stories about the ways other people's moms have died; how those people felt; and describing, in detail, the raw stage of grief. It seems, according to the news coverage, that the tidal wave of grief you are experiencing will be endless and unrelenting.

Neither of these is a good scenario. One is silence. The other is hyper-focused on a very tiny sliver of trauma.

When a parent dies, you may feel a period of immediate, intense grief. Your workplace and colleagues will usually respond with compassion and empathy, and perhaps a series of hot meals delivered to your home. Maybe you access bereavement leave to attend the funeral. Your colleagues all sign a card. They understand that you sometimes feel sad at work and are juggling a lot of logistics as you sell her house, deal with hospital bills, and administer her estate.

But life does go on, and you have to live without your mom for the rest of it. You want your colleagues to remember that Mother's Day is a rough day for you. You feel left out when coworkers talk about the grandparents visiting and babysitting the kids over the weekend. You need people to know that June 8 is a hard day for you because it was your mom's birthday. Or there is some stupid warm-up question about your favorite lunch as a kid, and you can't think of any happy thoughts about it because it reminds you of all the lunches your mom packed for you growing up.

The same is true for survivors of sexual violence. Our tendency is to focus on a very tiny sliver of a survivor's experience: the incident of harassment or the abuse itself. While believing survivors and supporting them through an incident and its immediate aftermath are critical, our roles as friends, partners, and colleagues don't end there.

After the incident and the immediate crisis that follows, victims live the rest of their lives as survivors. Being a survivor means different things for different people. For me, it meant feeling awkward when people talked about summer vacations growing up, since summer was when we visited family members who molested me. Do I make something up? Do I pass on a seemingly impersonal question? Do I chime in with the truth and disclose my history? It meant feeling alone when public stories about sexual abuse or assault broke on the media. Sometimes, I'd be up late at night following social media hashtags and feeling emotionally overwhelmed—which affected my focus and energy at work the next day. Friends and colleagues rarely check in during those moments, which mean less to them than they do to me. Other survivors might feel unsafe at certain bars, when they hear particular songs, or at certain times of day. They just want to be able to share why June 8 is hard for them, if it's the day they were sexually assaulted.

In a professional setting, it might mean preferring a seat with my back to the wall or staying out of conversations about childhood experiences because I don't want to bring the conversation down. Even just sharing a sideways glance with someone who understands my background when the topic comes up can be helpful. Knowing that people see you matters.

After #MeToo, employees asked me what to do or say if they had seen something online or on social media about a colleague's personal experience. Others reflected on how they might have discussed public cases of sexual assault in ways that could have sounded insensitive to survivors.

As a colleague or even a friend, supporting survivors doesn't have to mean hashing through the details of their assault or abuse. It just means being open to hearing and learning about how those experiences affected their lives and to seeing the whole picture so that we can build workplaces that allow survivors to contribute their talents and bring the skills they learned through healing to bear in a professional setting.

Finally, when considering the whole picture of survivors, it is essential to see beyond trauma to healing and resilience. With supportive friends, accepting communities, and professional guidance, many, many survivors are able to live their lives to their full potential. Some of the gifts they bring they've earned through survival and the hard work of healing, and those gifts benefit their friends, colleagues, and workplaces.

THE FRAMEWORK IN ACTION

Now that we've covered all five principles of the Framework, let's take a look at how they come together in a fictionalized conversation. Giovanni, a middle-aged manager in a warehouse, approached me after a workshop at a conference and asked if we could set up a call. During the workshop, he mentioned his family, the challenges of being a non-native English speaker, and confessed at one point that he hadn't spent much time thinking about the topic of sexual harassment.

As is often the case, I had no idea of what Giovanni wanted to talk about. Sometimes people want to ask me a policy question. At other times they disclose that they are victims of childhood sexual abuse. Still others have a practical question about their own behavior, or have a friend who needs advice. When we get on the phone, we do a little small talk, and then I jump right in. With Giovanni, I simply asked: "What's going on and how can I help?"

"Well, this weird thing has been happening," Giovanni responded. "You see, I work with mostly men, but there are a few women as well. One of the women is great at editing slides, and so sometimes, when I'm working on a presentation, I'll ask for her help. When she comes to my office, she closes the door, and instead of sitting down in my seat to look at my computer, she leans over me, really close. Like, she presses her whole body against my back. And then, instead of just moving the mouse, she puts her hand on top of mine to move it."

At this point in our conversation, I wasn't entirely sure where he was going. Was Giovanni going to confide in me about the start of a consensual workplace affair? Was he concerned about his own behavior or hers? I noted my own discomfort, but continued the conversation with more questions.

"Hmm," I said. "So how do you feel when this happens?"

"Really uncomfortable," Giovanni said. "I freeze. I just don't know what to do. It happened once, and I froze. And then it happened again, and so now I really don't know what to do. So I was hoping you could help me. What can I do?"

"Well, what do you want to happen?" I asked.

"I want it to stop. I want her to not do it again. But I'm worried about what might happen if I say something. Like, she could get mad, or she could say I was doing something to her. What should I say to make her stop?"

Like many people who approach me about issues at work, Giovanni seemed to be hoping I'd give him the magic words to fix the situation. I laughed a little and said, "So basically, you're hoping I could tell you the exact right thing to do or say? I wish I could, but, unfortunately, there are so many variables here that only you can decide the next right steps. But I can ask you a few questions that might help you consider some options. Is that okay?"

When he agreed, I asked, "Have you told anyone about it?"

"No, you're the first person I've told."

"Okay. Has your company provided any training on sexual harassment or how to behave at work?" I asked. When he said no, I asked if he had any other concerns, and Giovanni admitted that he was afraid his wife would find out and be angry.

As we continued to talk, the situation became clearer to me, and I hope to him, too. While Giovanni described the behavior that made him uncomfortable, he was unaware that it was likely covered by his company's sexual harassment policy. In fact, Giovanni knew very little about the definitions of sexual harassment or how his company handled it. He wasn't sure what he wanted to do next and was very concerned that he would somehow get in trouble at work or at home if others knew about these incidents.

The other important element here was that Giovanni didn't seem at all traumatized or afraid for his personal safety. He was only afraid of the personal and financial repercussions if he spoke up. While he had experienced sexual harassment, he also had more relative power than, say, if he had been a junior female employee whose male boss was touching her inappropriately when they were alone. It was also clear to me that his company wasn't doing all it could to prevent these kinds of incidents from taking place.

In this case, the whole-picture perspective required me to recognize and accept my role in what would be a series of conversations. There was nothing I could solve or fix in this conversation, or even in the broader context of Giovanni's life and experience. I'm not a counselor. I'm not an advocate for employees in workplace settings. This was a first conversation, so my role was really to help him talk through future conversations he could have about this issue, which is what we did. Here's what we covered:

- He could do nothing.

- He could attempt to avoid future interactions with this woman.

- He could say something directly to his colleague. This would require him knowing what to say, practicing it, and accepting the risks that come along with speaking up.

- He could talk to someone internally at his company, either about the situation or about sexual harassment training more broadly. We brainstormed who that might be, and whether there were others he trusted who might have wisdom to share.

- He could talk to someone externally who could advise him on his options.

- He could get support. If he was worried about talking to his wife, he could start with a hotline or professional counselor to get some insight and guidance.

I followed up with additional details on some of these resources, and wished him well.

It's important to note that this conversation was grounded in knowing facts about sexual harassment, which helped me continue to respond in appropriate ways. For example, Giovanni's gender didn't make it unlikely that he was being harassed. In fact, I was able to recognize that Giovanni's English skills put him in a less powerful position in certain dynamics. I also knew that Giovanni was acting like a normal person who experiences sexual harassment. It's normal to freeze and not know what to say. It's normal to hope something inappropriate doesn't happen again. He shouldn't need to tell this woman to keep her hands to herself. She should know not to do it.

My uncomfortable conversation with Giovanni certainly didn't resolve the situation immediately, but it did provide several benefits.

- Giovanni was able to break the ice in a supportive environment, which will set him up for future conversations about the incident or policy within his company.

- Giovanni and I both practiced a disclosure conversation— he disclosed and I responded.

- The conversation gave me further insight into how men experience sexual harassment, and some of the obstacles they face in reporting incidents and seeking support to deal with them.

- If Giovanni decides to inquire about sexual harassment policy at his company, he'll build his company's skill at conversations as well.

Will this single conversation ensure that Giovanni is never harassed again? No. Will this single conversation ensure that his company will protect all employees against harassment? No. That's not the point. The point is that we're both now in the habit of discussing these things—even if there is no immediate resolution, solution, or conclusion in the conversation. That's the way breaking the silence habit works. It's a series of conversations, not just one. Each conversation is important, but doesn't have to address every single perspective, solution, or issue.

Because I had given Giovanni and others at that workshop the language to explain the various elements of uncomfortable conversations, he could see them and name them when they arose. What's more, he had the courage to have an uncomfortable conversation about a work issue with me, a relative stranger. The more people within an organization feel grounded in the understanding and importance of uncomfortable conversations, the easier it becomes to initiate these conversations and continue having them. That's essential if you want to create a culture that will be resistant to sexual harassment and other forms of sexual violence.

Now that we've covered all five elements of The Uncomfortable Conversation Framework, we can move on to Part III, "Putting Conversations into Practice." In Chapter 8 we'll examine some specific benefits of practice conversations. In the remainder of Part III, we'll discuss putting the Framework into practice in situations like helpful interventions, supporting survivors, and dealing with power differentials.

CHAPTER SUMMARY

▶ The Whole Picture perspective opens up a host of possible conversations that are more focused on prevention, reflect the role of gender, and recognize the effect of sexual abuse and assault on our day-to-day work lives.

▶ The Whole Incident: Conversations about incidents of sexual harassment can reflect the experience and perspective of the person affected by harassment, the person who perpetrated it, and the people who could have prevented it from taking place.

▶ The Whole Gender: Seeing beyond the lens of our own gender requires us to consider the ways our gender impacts our behavior and relationships at work.

▶ The Whole Survivor: When we understand survivors more fully, we can see the ways their trauma and healing may show up in the workplace.

PART III

PUTTING CONVERSATIONS INTO PRACTICE

CHAPTER 8

THE POWER OF PRACTICE

CHOOSING CONVERSATION OVER SILENCE

One reason people avoid initiating uncomfortable conversations is the fear that they will result in an emotional blowup. What if I say something and they laugh it off? What if someone gets in trouble and their friends are angry at me? What if nothing is going on and they think I'm a party pooper? What if speaking up makes things worse?

In the case of uncomfortable conversations, an emotional reaction can feel awful in the moment. Even today, I can viscerally remember the first conversation with my mom about being molested and how terrified I was about her potential reaction. Nobody wants an explosion that turns into an angry confrontation or hurt feelings. However, this fear is an important sign of unpracticed conversations about all sorts of topics that need to be brought into the light, like boundaries, power, healthy relationships, and what constitutes appropriate behavior in the workplace.

If we want to create organizations—and communities—free of sexual harassment and violence, we have to map these emotional land mines and teach more people how to strategically and intentionally dismantle them. We must also teach people how to survive the moment when you set one off. When we treat unpracticed conversations like explosive devices that can kill us, we avoid them as though our lives depended on it. The truth is that we just need some more practice, both with the topic and with handling our own emotional responses to it.

Even speaking up about seemingly insignificant things can provoke intense emotional reactions. One time, I spoke to a colleague about a late night of drinking and rowdy conversation with junior colleagues, suggesting it might be inappropriate. The conversation blew up in my face after it was repeated and reinterpreted throughout the organization without any open communication or feedback. Even though nobody was harmed or even in trouble, that single conversation revealed numerous organizational challenges around trust, feedback, policy, and managerial expectations. It caused conflict with my colleagues when we realized we were on different pages about what constituted appropriate workplace behavior and how to best respond to something like this.

I've replayed that conversation a thousand times, wondering if a different script or approach might have led to a different result. It's certainly possible. Knowing the outcome, if I had it to do over again, I'd probably try a different tactic. And I know I'll probably overcorrect myself the next time a situation like this occurs. I regret the impact of the conversation on my colleague and others in the organization who heard about it third- or fourth-hand; however, I don't regret the conversation at all.

Would I stay silent next time?

No way.

Even when a conversation about sexual harassment or violence doesn't go as planned, it almost always has a positive impact on the culture when approached through The Uncomfortable Conversation Framework. In this case, the conversation broke the ice on a topic that deserved further discussion, and provided everyone involved with a chance to practice and get better at uncomfortable conversations. The conflicts, while painful in the moment, eventually calmed down and we could all get back to work.

Over time, I've learned that a messy emotional explosion won't kill me. It's uncomfortable, like going on a run. It doesn't feel great in the moment, but the effects are undoubtedly positive—both for me personally, and for the organization or culture.

In the situation in my organization, I chose conversation over silence after something troubling took place. At the time, those in my organization were unaware of the role, purpose, or framing of uncomfortable conversations. Imagine how the entire incident might have unfolded had we shared a collective understanding of uncomfortable conversations.

To take it one step further, imagine if we had already engaged in conversations about drinking, socializing, and boundaries prior to this late-night gathering. Our conversation would have had a prior context and we might have understood each other's perspectives more fully—outside of a more urgent situation. The Uncomfortable Conversation Framework gives us the confidence to start conversations about sexual harassment and violence, instead of just engaging reactively. Now that you have the framing, and hopefully some more confidence, this section of the book will provide you with the tools you need to practice, and then initiate, several kinds of critical conversations that help to prevent and respond to sexual harassment and violence in the workplace more effectively.

THE HOW AND WHY OF PRACTICE CONVERSATIONS

When we practice conversations within organizations or communities, we can achieve several goals. First, we can get better at recognizing reaction-prone topics and learn how to approach them with caution. Second, we can begin to systematically scan the behavioral and relationship hot spots that exist within ourselves and in our team before they erupt. Finally, we can work through some of the challenges in these conversations around fictional people and scenarios, which hold much lower stakes for us than real people in real organizations.

Knowing we won't usually get do-overs means that we have to

find ways to practice uncomfortable conversations ahead of time. Practice won't guarantee that we can avoid complicated, emotional reactions, but it does give us a chance to map out potential conversational and emotional challenges we might provoke. When we practice with a broad group of colleagues, we learn who has experience and who might struggle with finding the right words. We learn how to give and receive feedback about our behavior. We learn about each other's boundaries. We begin to see the organization through the eyes of people who have more or less power than we do, which allows us to intervene more effectively.

The idea that we'll be able to engage in perfect, magical, comfortable conversations about a topic as complicated and taboo as sexual harassment is a complete myth. We are going to mess it up, get it wrong, and learn things every time we do it. Why wait until a high-stakes situation emerges to make mistakes? By intentionally practicing in a low-stakes environment, with a focus on the conversations that need to take place *before* an incident, we build individual and organizational skills and gain the experience we need to better handle incidents that do emerge.

Practicing uncomfortable conversations grounded in realistic scenarios tailored for your workplace offers you and your team many benefits.

- Practice prepares you to handle common scenarios and dynamics that affect healthy relationships, boundaries, and behavior in the workplace. You will have a sense both of what you might say, and of how your colleagues might respond and why. This knowledge lowers the emotional volatility of future conversations that will inevitably arise.

- Practice inspires more uncomfortable conversations. Breaking the ice is often the hardest thing to do. It's like taking people on their first run. Once you realize that the discomfort gives way to a feeling of exhilaration and freedom, you are more likely to try it out again.

- Practice moves your team away from the idea of a one-size-fits-all behavior or language and illustrates the diversity of perspectives within a single group or organization. People become less likely to unintentionally say or do something that will make their colleagues feel unsafe or disrespected.

- Practice makes this issue real in a way that statistics and policies do not. When we practice conversations around fictional scenarios, we imagine ourselves and our colleagues in them and begin to understand the real emotional and practical impact of sexual harassment in the workplace.

- Practice raises the underlying issues that need to be addressed. If policies aren't clear, or if your colleagues have trouble setting or respecting boundaries, or if no one trusts human resources, it's better to know this before an incident takes place.

- Practice reveals how much practice is still needed and the skills that may be lacking on your team. When you are aware of your limitations or see how new skills might make it easier to respond to common scenarios, you are more likely to invest in your own growth.

- Practice leads to lifelong habits around uncomfortable conversations that are critical to creating long-term cultural change.

A practice conversation means unpacking a "what if" scenario with others in your organization. You consider a case study and discuss what you would do "as if" you were in that situation yourself. Approaching a conversation with an uncomfortable conversation mindset allows you to discuss and reflect on two things: ways to respond to incidents or suspected incidents and to consider the silence—or lack of conversation—that led to the incident in the first place. You can try this with the following case study.

CASE STUDY **THE NAKED MUD WRESTLING VIDEO**

Before you start practicing on your own, let's walk through a scenario I've workshopped with dozens of different groups to see what practice looks like in the context of helpful intervention. The scenario is relatively simple and straightforward.

Ray walks by a mixed-gender group of employees laughing at something on the screen. As Ray gets closer, he sees that they're watching a YouTube video of naked mud wrestling.

Ray has several options. He can approach the group and intervene. He can report the incident to human resources. He can talk to someone about it after the fact and then decide what to do. Or he can stay quiet and do nothing at all. What should Ray do next?

In a practice conversation, the idea isn't to figure out the "right answer." Instead, it's to create a conversation with a colleague or group of colleagues about all the possible responses and the reasons behind them. By avoiding your natural instinct to figure out the perfect solution, you've created an immediate opportunity to dive into the discomfort of not knowing exactly what to say or do.

Your personal response will likely fall into one of the following categories:

- Ray should do nothing.

- Ray should intervene.

- Ray should report to a manager.

- Ray should *not* report to a manager.

CASE STUDY, *cont.*

But this isn't a multiple-choice exam—it's a conversation. Your response may be the same as your conversation partner or the colleagues in your group. Either way, the next question is the same: "Why?"

Asking "why" begins the process of unpacking the assumptions and skills you bring to a particular scenario, and discussing your "why" with colleagues provides opportunities for each of you to learn from the others. When conversations about scenarios like this are practiced in a group, the dialogue is rich in learning and skill development. When I workshopped this scenario with one group of employees at a technology company, several of them asserted that watching videos of naked mud wrestling wasn't in violation of their company's policy. This provided an opportunity for the management team to clarify that videos involving nudity were, in fact, in violation of company policy, even if they were not explicitly pornographic. This was not a gray area for this particular company. In addition to this assertion, the company also reminded employees that content viewed in the workplace and on work-provided computers was covered by company policy, even if the viewing happened outside of work hours. This information was surprising to several employees—they did not have the facts necessary. The response to the scenario—and the why—provided an opportunity to clarify a factual misunderstanding. If you don't know or fully understand the rules, you may not follow them or feel empowered to enforce them with colleagues. This discussion also provided employees who understood that nudity was in violation of company policy a chance to pause their reaction and allow those new facts into the conversation.

Of course, if yours is a company that produces videos about naked mud wrestling or works with partners who engage with risqué content, it could just be a regular Tuesday night at the office. If this is the case, the scenario might lead

CASE STUDY, *cont.*

to a different conversation about where this kind of content is viewed, whether it's possible to avoid seeing it, and how employees are trained and onboarded. At the technology company, one employee recalled a previous employer that provided private spaces to view sensitive content when it was part of someone's job responsibilities.

Let's consider some other reasons you might not intervene. For example, you may not consider mud wrestling to be porn. This is a common reason behind not intervening, and slightly different from it not being explicitly against policy. Maybe you wouldn't think to report the behavior or intervene simply because it's not offensive to you personally. If this is the case, your colleagues might ask some follow-up questions: Might someone else be offended by the content? Why or why not? Does everyone have a right to go to work and not be offended?

Other people were laughing, including women. If you assume laughter means approval, you can continue to unpack that assumption further as well. Can you think of a time that you laughed for a reason other than a situation being funny? What about discomfort? Going along with the group? Fitting in? A video being funny is just one of many reasons why someone might be laughing.

Perhaps you wouldn't intervene because *intervention didn't seem possible.* Unpacking this response might lead to several important insights about employee behavior and organizational culture. For example, the underlying issue could be receptivity to feedback. If you think the group would have an angry response to feedback, it makes total sense that you wouldn't intervene. An inability to receive feedback affects not just a situation like this but might also impact other aspects of workplace culture and productivity.

Alternatively, you might just lack the skills to intervene, either in that moment or at all. If you can't imagine what Ray might say in this scenario, chances are that you don't have the right words, either. If you don't have the skill—or the power—then not intervening might seem like the best choice in the moment. Even if you think Ray should intervene, you don't always know why or how he should do so.

These initial responses—and questions—help transition the conversation into a more practical brainstorming and skill-building session around bystander intervention, with opportunities to point out how different power dynamics, genders, and personalities come into play. There is no single way to respond, and it always depends on the relationship between Ray and the other employees, and Ray's personal style. In Ray's place, you might decide to address the entire group directly in the moment, while others might approach the person they know the best after the fact. While one person might offer a gentle reminder about company policy, another might use humor to intervene—or distract the group by inviting them out for drinks. There might be disagreement about the "right" way to intervene, but it's important to remember that intervention skills are developed over time.

While working together as a group or a team, you can brainstorm possibilities for what someone could do or say in the moment, which will help you benefit from the collective skill in the group. When we brainstormed ideas at the technology company, we came up with quite a few possible responses.

- Hey there, what *is* that?

- You know, a bunch of female colleagues at my last company quit because people watched stuff like this.

- #NSFW much? (Not Suitable For Work)

- Could you turn that off?

CASE STUDY, *cont.*

- Why don't you wrap that up? Pretty sure Jay (the CEO) wouldn't want you to be watching that, and he's still in the office.

- Guys, I guess you skipped the training on our company's harassment policy?

When we came up with these ideas, we played out the exchange a little further, and addressed some of the fears that arise about speaking up. When you think through a few additional comebacks, you'll feel more prepared if someone laughs it off or makes fun of you when you intervene in a higher-stakes, real-life situation. For example, "I'd rather be weak than fired," or "Joe, I think you may be out solo on this one, right, guys?"

This dissection of a single, relatively nonthreatening scenario gives you a chance to see how the guiding principles of The Uncomfortable Conversation Framework can help you navigate a conversation in a new way. Each time you do this with a group, you build specific skills around responding to disclosures of harassment, how and when to intervene, and the ways in which different genders and experiences might inform responses. You may also discover that you have questions about policy, can translate a skill from another experience in your life, or realize that you feel totally unprepared to respond in a particular way.

SKILLS GAINED THROUGH PRACTICE

The skill of the uncomfortable conversation, in turn, unlocks a series of additional skills that can be further developed through uncomfortable conversation practice. These skills will require you to both initiate conversations on your own and respond to conversations that others initiate.

As with any skill, practice makes perfect. That's why it's critical to practice in a low-stakes environment around fictional scenarios, in an environment that supports learning. As you move into practice, remember both that you are practicing a response to a scenario and also that the conversations leading up to the scenario could impact future responses.

The core skills that will be explored in the next three chapters include:

- **HELPFUL INTERVENTION.** Recognizing behavior along a spectrum and determining a strategy for intervening that is appropriate to the situation.

- **RECOGNIZING AND ADDRESSING POWER.** Reflecting on where power dynamics may be at play that affect workplace interactions and how they influence the impact of your behavior and words at work.

- **SETTING AND RESPECTING BOUNDARIES.** Understanding the role of personal and professional boundaries and how both setting them and respecting them can be challenging for some people.

- **RESPONDING TO AND SUPPORTING SURVIVORS AT WORK.** Learning how to respond compassionately—and legally— to someone who has experienced either sexual harassment in the workplace or sexual abuse or assault at another point in their lives.

These skills will be explored in greater depth in the next three chapters, along with practice conversations you can use with colleagues or with your team. Once you've reflected on your own responses, Chapter 12 also offers several ways you can engage your team or colleagues in practice conversations.

CHAPTER SUMMARY

▸ Once we embrace The Uncomfortable Conversation Framework, we become more confident in our ability to engage in conversations about sexual harassment and violence and, more important, to initiate conversations on our own.

▸ By practicing conversations, we bring potential obstacles to communicating effectively about particular scenarios to the surface and can even begin to recognize what conversations might prevent sexual harassment from happening in the first place.

▸ A case study discussion illustrates how a practice conversation works, the skills it helps to develop, and the benefits it brings to a group.

▸ Practice conversations help you build skills like helpful intervention, navigating power and boundaries, and responding to people who have experienced sexual harassment and violence.

CHAPTER 9

HELPFUL INTERVENTION

UNDERSTANDING IMPACT AND INTERVENTION

Initiating an uncomfortable conversation can feel especially intimidating. To do so effectively, it's necessary to recognize when troubling behavior is taking place, understand the role we play, and have the words to respond effectively in the moment. This concept is called bystander intervention, or helpful intervention.

Take this story as an example. In her early twenties, a friend of mine was working in a client-facing role at a company in a male-dominated industry. One night, she joined a group of senior colleagues for a dinner out with an important client. As the night progressed, the client began making flirty comments about her appearance, kept buying her drinks she hadn't asked for, moved to sit next to her at dinner, and began touching her lower back while they spoke. My friend was not interested in his advances, but recognized how important the client was to the company. As she looked around the table, her colleagues were laughing, joking, and enjoying their dinner.

Stories like these are common, and I hear about them both through the lens of people like my friend, the young and apparently single junior employee, and through the eyes of the more senior colleagues at the dinner. Why don't people speak up?

First, they lack situational awareness, or the ability to see the whole picture of the situation. As a result, they are more likely to view the behavior that is unfolding as a private, personal interaction—and respond with thoughts like these:

> *She shouldn't have dressed so provocatively. She's using her sexuality to close the deal. She should be careful.*

> *He's a creep. He should know better. Some guys are just jerks.*

When incidents of sexual harassment take place, we tend to view them through the lens of the individual—two people having a problematic interaction—rather than as a problem that actually impacts our entire organization and culture.

The truth is that dozens of people are affected by this inappropriate interaction. My friend is left thinking that her colleagues don't have her back. My friend's team is affected, especially the colleagues at the table who are disgusted by the behavior and distracted from the work at hand. Other employees at my friend's company who will have to interact with this person, perhaps alone, might also be subject to his inappropriate advances or worse, if nobody calls attention to it. Employees at other companies, now or in the future, who share this client will have to expend extra energy on managing a toxic person. Whether or not the incident is formally reported, the general counsel and human resources departments at both companies are impacted, because this individual has created a situation in which one or both companies might face liability.

When we see the depth and breadth of the impact of an incident like this, we are more likely to feel urgency around intervention and are able to engage others who are affected in the intervention itself.

The second reason people don't speak up is that they don't understand the purpose of helpful intervention. Behavior exists on a spectrum, ranging from completely healthy to violent and abusive.

When we consistently intervene on the less harmful end of the spectrum, we can actually help prevent violence from taking place. In this situation, when the client makes a flirty comment that isn't addressed, he is empowered by the silence to take his behavior one step further. Even if others at the table are disgusted, the client, the perpetrator of sexual harassment, doesn't know that unless they speak up. It requires less skill to intervene before a situation becomes unstable or violent, so the sooner an intervention takes place, the better for everyone involved. While we will, occasionally, witness or overhear something that is definitively sexual harassment, an unambiguous incident can't be our bar for intervention.

Finally, witnesses—or bystanders—don't always understand the tactics of bystander intervention. While it's one thing to engage in an uncomfortable conversation that someone else starts, it's another thing to break the ice yourself. Bystander intervention in the context of workplace harassment means that all employees proactively address words and behavior that might make the workplace unsafe for others. When we view silence as a choice, we can rank it against other options—and see that even spilling your drink on the handsy client might be a better option than keeping your mouth shut. Bystander intervention is not simply an intervention that directly stops one person's behavior. It's also an intervention on the unhealthy culture that allows that person to behave in inappropriate ways.

We can all be effective bystanders and cultural change agents, simply by first learning how to identify words and behaviors that could cause harm. Every day, you probably see, hear, and experience things in the workplace that are troubling in some way. To name a few:

- Off-color jokes or awkward compliments in the workplace
- A colleague walking out of a room crying
- A colleague commenting on another employee as creepy

- A colleague who is a close talker or particularly touchy-feely with others

- Comments about "all men" or "all women" in the context of workplace behavior

- Conversations about dating colleagues or bosses

- Someone intoxicated at a work event or conference

- Comments about the physical appearance or attractiveness of other employees

- A friend becoming irritable when a date or partner doesn't text back immediately

- Laughing off training about sexual harassment or misconduct

- Comments that might be offensive to survivors of sexual abuse or assault, making light of rape or its impact

As you can see, this is not a list of behaviors that constitute sexual harassment. It's a list of signals that something could be happening, or signs that people in your workplace environment may be vulnerable to harassment. These aren't necessarily situations where calling in the "authorities" is necessary, and that may not be possible in the moment anyway. But we can change the culture ourselves by taking action and initiating an uncomfortable conversation in the moment.

People don't initiate uncomfortable conversations for lots of reasons. They think it's none of their business. They don't want to risk relationships or cause a conflict. They might be afraid of an angry reaction or other forms of retaliation. Sometimes they aren't 100 percent sure what they saw or heard, or they don't know what to say and the moment passes. Sometimes they assume the person speaking was joking or is otherwise a nice person. If others are silent, they might assume everyone else thinks the behavior or statement is okay.

The hardest part of an uncomfortable conversation is starting it, which is why bystander intervention is called out as a distinct skill. Furthermore, research on bystander intervention in other contexts suggests that communities with engaged bystanders are more able to prevent sexual harassment and violence from taking place.[1] If you know how to engage in an uncomfortable conversation, you can recognize when it's necessary and learn how to start it.

TIPS FOR EFFECTIVE INTERVENTION

Effective intervention is highly dependent on both the situation and the person who is initiating it. There isn't one "right thing" to do or say. Your approach has to work with your personality and style. However, when you recognize behavior or statements that might require an intervention, your intervention will likely fall into one of four categories, summarized here from a broad range of programs and trainings.[2]

- **DIRECT.** This is what most of us think of as bystander intervention. It's speaking up directly to the person who is behaving in an inappropriate way. Direct intervention requires confidence and practice.

- **DISRUPT.** The goal of disruption is to stop the inappropriate conversation or behavior from continuing. This could be as dramatic as "accidentally" dropping a stack of papers to the ground or as simple as pointing out it's time for lunch.

- **DELEGATE.** If you are skilled at recognizing and addressing power, you can also consider engaging someone else to actually do the speaking up. Maybe it's someone who is bigger than you or has more situational power, or who has a stronger relationship with any party involved.

- **DELAY.** If you can't figure out a way to intervene in the moment, you can do so after the fact. This also requires finding a way to bring up the statement or behavior after the fact, which is another form of breaking the ice.

If the concept of bystander intervention intrigues you, there are many ways to improve your skills through additional training or programs. Through the practice conversations in this book, you will have a chance to try out bystander intervention and develop your own style and approach.

▶ I SAW SOMETHING. WHAT DO I SAY?

If you witness an incident of inappropriate or troubling behavior that you think may constitute sexual harassment, consider the following next steps:

- Intervene immediately, using one of the four D's (direct, disrupt, delegate, delay) of helpful intervention.

- Intervene after the incident by speaking privately to one or more of the participants.

- Report the behavior to your manager or to an internal human resources representative.

- Discuss the incident with a trusted colleague, probably a peer, to better understand what happened and what you ought to do next. Remember, if you or the colleague is a manager and is required to report, this may not be a confidential conversation.

- Discuss the incident with a trusted friend or neutral expert outside of the organization to better understand what happened and what you ought to do next.

Each of these options has advantages and disadvantages. If you intervene in the moment, someone might get defensive or angry. If you wait, there is more risk that a colleague might continue to feel unsafe.

PRACTICE CONVERSATION #1

INAPPROPRIATE COMMENTS

When you witness something objectively inappropriate, it can be really challenging to speak up. The next scenario, where direct and immediate intervention is appropriate, gives you a chance to practice what you might say and to try different styles of intervention. At the same time, this scenario allows you and your colleagues to explore additional options if immediate intervention doesn't seem possible. Finally, this scenario illustrates the connection between seemingly "small" comments and a culture that tolerates inappropriate behavior.

> Conversation Starter: *At a project meeting, Angelina gets up to grab a cup of coffee while discussing a major sale she just closed. As she turns around, Jose, her peer, comments with a smirk that she must have been wearing that outfit during the sales meeting. Angelina laughs it off and sits back down, actively participating in the rest of the meeting. What should you, another manager at the meeting, do in this situation?*

Possible Responses

- Address it in the moment with Jose.

- Address it privately with Jose.

- Follow up with Angelina after the meeting.

- Report the incident to human resources.

Discussion and Reflection Questions

- What's the impact of a comment like this on Angelina? Why might Jose have said something like this?

- What's the effect of a comment like this on other people in the room who witnessed it? What's the impact of managers staying silent in response? If comments like this are acceptable in public, what conclusions can we draw about things that are acceptable behind closed doors?

- What specifically might the manager say? How might the other person respond, and why?

- What if the comment was something less overt? Like a comment about her winning smile?

- If the comment isn't addressed by the manager, what role might other employees play? Who else might approach Jose (or Angelina), and what might they say?

- Why might this incident be reported? What is the impact of it being reported or not reported? What if Angelina doesn't want to report it? (Answers may vary widely depending on whether your organization requires reporting incidents like these.)

- How might this situation look or feel different if the scenario were written with different genders?

For each discussion question, challenge yourself to go one level deeper by asking yourself or your conversation partner to share why they gave the response they gave. Additionally, ask yourself what conversations might have prevented this situation from taking place or what could minimize the effect of something like this happening in the future.

Benefits of Conversation

- Practice key strategies around bystander intervention that may be useful in other situations.

- Learn how and why your colleagues might respond in similar or different ways to the same incident.

- Consider the ways silence or laughter in the face of inappropriate comments impacts trust in the organization, managers, and policies.

PRACTICE CONVERSATION #2

NOT TAKING TRAINING SERIOUSLY

Conversations about sexual harassment are uncomfortable, and people deal with discomfort in different ways. While humor is one way of dealing with discomfort, it can also come across as insensitive, especially without context. This scenario encourages you and your colleagues to explore why you think training is useful, and how you deal with discomfort and healthy or unhealthy expressions of humor. This scenario also explores the role of peer pressure and assumptions we make about groups of people interacting together.

> Conversation Starter: *Ari's company is rolling out a new online sexual harassment training, a requirement for all employees. They walk by a colleague's desk to see a group of guys gathered around a computer screen and laughing. When they look closer, they see that the guys are making fun of the training slides. What should Ari do next?*

Possible Responses

- Ari should say something in the moment.

- Ari should report the incident to their manager or human resources.

- Ari should approach one person in the group privately.

- Ari should ask another colleague who is closer to the group to approach them.

As with the previous scenario, deepen the conversation around each reflection question by digging into the "why" behind the response, and don't forget to consider the kinds of conversations that might prevent a scenario like this from unfolding the way it did.

Discussion and Reflection Questions

- Why might the guys be laughing? What emotions or situations might cause people to laugh? What might be on the slides that could provoke laughter? Is laughing during a serious topic allowable?

- What specifically might Ari say to the guys? How might they respond?

- What specifically might Ari say to human resources? How might they respond? What questions might they ask?

- Are there any other people—either described explicitly or not—who might be able to help with effective intervention? Who might they be? How might Ari engage them to help?

- What is the impact of laughter on Ari? On other people who might hear it or hear about it later? What intentional or unintentional messages might the laughter send?

- How might Ari's gender affect their response or the response of their colleagues?

Benefits of Conversation

- Highlights the difference between a reaction and what may be going on underneath. People laugh for all sorts of reasons. The training could be dumb or remind them of the latest *Saturday Night Live* skit. The people could be uncomfortable.

- Highlights the impact of sexual harassment. For people who have experienced harassment directly, the training may be a serious matter where laughter seems insulting.

- Introduces the role of positive and negative peers and their influence on our behavior.

- Offers an opportunity to practice intervention in a more advanced setting—intervening with a group is a higher-level skill.

- Creates space to critique previous trainings about sexual harassment. Employees may laugh at training that is ineffective or unrealistic.

CHAPTER SUMMARY

▶ When it comes to sexual harassment and violence, behavior ranges from healthy and consensual to violent and aggressive. The earlier on the spectrum of behavior that we intervene, the less likely we are to enable behavior that is violent and aggressive.

▶ Incidents of sexual harassment impact more than just the people involved; they affect the organization. When we can recognize the broader impact of sexual harassment, we are more likely to intervene, knowing we will likely have the support of our colleagues.

▶ Helpful intervention can incorporate four key strategies: direct, disrupt, delegate, and delay.

▶ Practice conversations provide an opportunity to understand helpful intervention and the approaches you and your colleagues might utilize in the moment.

CHAPTER 10

POWER AND BOUNDARIES

RECOGNIZING AND ADDRESSING POWER

You may have heard the phrase "Sexual harassment and violence are about power, not about sex." Understanding power—who has it, why they have it, and how they use it, intentionally or unintentionally—is a critical element of prevention and response. Power is relative based on the dominant culture and groups, so it can vary from team to team and organization to organization.

Oftentimes, we see power as something that happens *to* us, rather than as a set of systems we participate in together. When we see power in this way, we miss out on chances to wield our own power, individually or collectively, in positive ways. When we can't see our own relative power, we rely on the people who have the least amount of power to defend themselves against harassment and violence. Sometimes people don't speak up because they don't perceive their own power.

If you are in a position of power, it's up to you to understand various interactions and scenarios from the perspective of someone with less power. Power is often invisible to those who have it. I'll often ask male professionals whether they have ever felt scared at work. The answer is usually no. This isn't the case for people of other genders, and learning this can be really valuable to male managers who don't normally think about their physical safety in the context of commuting, work-related travel, or other projects on the job. When a newly promoted manager suddenly realizes that her words carry more weight in meetings and that she has influence over decisions that impact her colleagues, this discovery can be both intoxicating and uncomfortable. In either case, it requires skill to use power in a new way. People in power have to choose their words, monitor their behavior, and find ways to tolerate the scrutiny that comes with power.

Power manifests itself within organizations in many ways that go beyond gender. For example:

- People in upper-level positions or people who supervise others.

- People in positions that control benefits, resources, or perks. (For example, the person in charge of scheduling shifts may not be the highest-ranking person in the organization, but controls something important to a lot of employees.)

- People who are heterosexual and are in relationships with people of the opposite gender.

- People who are physically bigger, stronger, or are free of physical or mental disability.

- People whose gender, racial, and cultural identities match that of the majority of the organization.

- People who speak the dominant language of the company.

Power, in and of itself, is not bad. When power is used responsibly and safely, it can add momentum to ideas, projects, and industries. It's challenging only when we don't recognize our own power and the role it plays in relationships. It's destructive only when we hoard power unto ourselves without sharing it with others. We need to build skills that let us speak honestly and productively about the challenges that come with having power, not just about the challenges of being powerless. The practice of

POWER DYNAMICS AND HARASSMENT

When harassment is perpetrated by people outside of the organization by sales prospects, investors, or vendors, the power dynamics shift, and therefore the conversations shift as well. Scenarios exploring third-party harassment give us a chance to practice talking about power and its role in sexual harassment prevention. In many cases, the offenders may be in positions of power.

This example is written for sales, but it could also be explored for supervisors, vendors, clients, or investors.

Conversation Starter: *Franco's direct report, Deidre, confesses that one of her sales prospects made an aggressive pass at her earlier that week. They were alone in a conference room, and, without warning, he pinned her against the wall and tried to kiss her. The incident scared Deidre pretty badly, but she is close to securing a major sale and doesn't want to make a big deal out of it. How should Franco respond?*

Possible Responses

- Franco should do nothing.

- Franco should advise Deidre on how to stay safe at the next meeting.

- Franco should immediately take her off the account.

- Franco should go with her to the next meeting with the sales prospect.

- Franco should talk to the sales prospect directly.

- Franco should talk to someone else, either at the company or at the prospect's company.

Reflection and Discussion Questions

- Why might Deidre not want to make a big deal out of this situation? How might reporting impact her compensation, performance, professional growth, or future job prospects?

- Why might Franco follow Deidre's wishes or choose a response that could be in conflict with her wishes? What role does a victim's individual preference play in relationship to safety for others who may come in contact with a perpetrator?

- What responsibilities does Franco have as a manager? What policies might inform Franco's response?

- Who is responsible for Deidre's safety? What are the ways she can stay safe? What role can Franco play? Are there roles for people not mentioned in the scenario?

- Who might be in the best position to intervene with the sales prospect? Who has power or influence over the sales prospect? How might that person be engaged?

- What might Deidre need to know in order to feel more secure reporting an incident like this to her supervisor? What conversations might they have had that would have led her to conclude it was best to "not make a big deal" out of what happened?

As with all practice conversations, take a moment to unpack your response and the response of your conversation partners to better understand their perspectives, and how power dynamics might influence their reactions or approaches.

Benefits of Conversation

- Provides insights into executive perspective on harassment by investors and sales prospects. This practice conversation offers executives a chance to say that they will stand up for their employees in situations like this.

- Offers an opportunity to view power from different angles and consider how power affects our choices about responding to sexual harassment and misconduct.

- Illustrates how the wishes of victims may sometimes be in tension with company policy around reporting, and what might be behind reporting hesitation.

- Gives new insights into the safety issues facing employees who regularly interact with people outside of the organization.

- Clarifies policies related to mandated or obligated reporting for managers, and gives all employees a chance to better understand the role of those policies.

uncomfortable conversations—particularly when it comes to asking practical questions and seeing the whole picture—gives us the opportunity to better see and understand power and how it affects behavior, boundaries, and relationships at work.

SETTING AND RESPECTING BOUNDARIES

When I was presenting a scenario about unclear boundaries and communication, the group discussion began to get heated. The scenario described a situation where Mike invited Michelle for drinks several times, after Michelle politely declined. Michelle felt uncomfortable and reported the situation to a manager. This scenario, which you will have an opportunity to practice later in the chapter, is intentionally vague to illustrate how challenging it can be to set boundaries clearly and recognize when a boundary is being set.

Initially, a woman in the workshop wondered aloud about the degree to which Michelle was clear and direct in declining the invitation.

"Did she just say *sorry, I'm busy* or did she tell Mike to stop inviting her out?"

"Yeah, I mean, you can't just be vague and then get upset. That's not fair," chimed in a male colleague.

A voice full of emotion interrupted from across the room: "Doesn't Michelle deserve to have her NO respected? She shouldn't have to say no multiple times."

At this point, as the facilitator, I paused the conversation. Predictably, the scenario evoked strong reactions and differing points of view. The underlying tension, which the scenario is designed to illuminate, is the varying skill and style individuals bring to setting and respecting boundaries in the workplace. For some people, setting a boundary is easy and the words roll off their tongue, even in difficult moments. For others, setting a boundary is terrifying, especially when they feel uncomfortable or threatened. In responding to this scenario, someone who struggles to set boundaries might sound different than someone who doesn't.

Engaging in the practice of uncomfortable conversations helps employees better understand and negotiate boundaries, which is a core skill in a culture that is free of sexual harassment. Setting and respecting boundaries is something we do frequently in our day-to-day lives across a variety of circumstances. When you visit a colleague's office, you don't take a pen out of their hand or start typing notes on their computer unless you're asked. At the same time, you can also relate to how hard it can be to tell a chatty, extroverted colleague to be quiet when you are working on a project with a fast-approaching deadline.

When it comes to personal and emotional space, setting and respecting boundaries becomes even more complicated and can feel risky. Unfortunately, it is often not until a boundary has been crossed, or at least approached, that we realize we may have to draw one. This can make drawing boundaries challenging. For instance, if someone asks whether you plan to have children, and you are in the midst of an emotionally challenging series of fertility treatments or pregnancy attempts and you don't want to talk about it, you then have to either draw a boundary and say, "Oh, that's really a private issue, but thank you for asking," or avoid the conversation. But avoiding the conversation at that point doesn't let the person know it's an off-limits topic for you.

Setting boundaries requires us to give people feedback on their behavior, which can also be uncomfortable for the person having a boundary drawn on them. When you respond to a question about having kids by saying, "I don't want to talk about it," you've given feedback to the person who asked the question. The colleague who asked the question might feel embarrassed for having spoken, wonder whether they phrased the question correctly, or find it difficult to understand why you're so sensitive about the topic—especially if they haven't experienced fertility challenges.

Respecting boundaries is a skill. Some people are adept at reading social cues; they know when a subject or a question is making the person they're talking to uncomfortable, and how to back out of the conversation gracefully. Other people seem to have blinders on and can't understand why a certain joke or subject causes someone to start avoiding them in the cafeteria. In the example about setting a boundary about an infertility conversation, one colleague might respond with an apology for bringing up the topic in the first place while another might criticize you for being so sensitive in your response.

Because we each have our own unique personal backgrounds and boundaries, conversations about those boundaries can sometimes be uncomfortable. Practicing uncomfortable conversations gives us a chance to learn about where boundary hot spots may exist in relationships and organizations. While policies help with defining some of the lines, we also have to learn to protect and respect our individual lines around personal and emotional space. If someone doesn't want to be touched at work, and you are someone who uses touch to make a point, both of you are going to have to work on reminding each other and learning. Often we assume that people have either perfectly good intentions or horribly bad intentions when a boundary is crossed. Uncomfortable conversations can help us identify the people who cross boundaries on purpose, those who lack the social skills to recognize boundaries but don't mean harm, and people who have different ideas about personal boundaries than we do.

For example, at one training, a woman shared that she always refused to ride in the back seat with sales prospects when they rode together in a ride-share or taxi. This wasn't a company policy by any means; it was a personal preference that helped her feel safer while traveling for work. It also provided an opportunity for her to test how the sales prospect responded to having a boundary set. Someone who easily respects boundaries might respond by saying,

"Of course, whatever makes you feel comfortable." Someone else might be offended that she didn't want to sit closer, or might try to insist that she do something that made her feel uncomfortable. All of this informed her future decisions about how to interact with the prospect. She felt empowered to set these boundaries because her manager backed her up, and she discussed them openly with others on her team as well.

When we talk about being more assertive in the workplace with people who are crossing boundaries, it can sometimes sound as though we are blaming victims of boundary violations for not being assertive enough. This is not the case. If this woman, for some reason, sat in the back of the car with someone who groped her, *it would never be her fault.* The truth is, we can teach people to become more skillful at setting boundaries while still requiring that boundaries be respected by others. These are two separate skills.

Talking about boundaries in the context of sexual harassment can be especially tricky. In a healthy organization, individuals will have skills around setting and respecting boundaries. But the individual skill isn't enough. The boundaries must also be supported by the organization through effective policy development, implementation, and support.

At the organizational level, policies are boundaries that can be designed to help people act appropriately around one another and consequently make the workplace feel safe for everyone. For example, sometimes women are praised for being able to "handle" inappropriate jokes and inappropriate people. They may even be proud of themselves for doing so. However, the organization also plays a role in ensuring that its employees are protected and safe. When an organization sets a boundary through a policy, it takes the onus of boundary-setting off the shoulders of those who are vulnerable and invites others to participate in the work of setting a boundary around appropriate behavior. Policies around workplace relationships, alcohol, and safety in the workplace may seem to be set around relatively minor behaviors, but those policies are designed to prevent harmful behavior and maintain the safety of those with the least amount of power in the organization. However, these boundary-setting policies won't work unless everyone understands their purpose and helps enforce them.

This brings us back to the need for more conversation and skill-building around boundaries. Three separate and distinct, but important principles are related to boundaries.

1. Teach people to set boundaries before harm takes place.

2. Use boundary-setting to identify people who can't respect boundaries.

3. Test and monitor people's skills around setting and respecting boundaries through both practice conversations and policies.

Boundary-setting requires communications skills, confidence, and the lived experience of knowing your boundaries will be respected. If you've been taught that assertiveness is bad and being polite is essential, you may be hesitant to set boundaries.

Respecting boundaries requires a recognition of power dynamics, empathy for other people, and an openness to feedback. If you can't hear the word "no" without getting angry or hurt, you're going to have trouble respecting the boundaries of others. If you think that pushing the line is a fun game, you might not be able to see it when someone gets hurt when you push over the line.

When it comes to boundaries, we bring diverse perspectives to the table. Take the case of the degree to which a boundary can be drawn around work hours. Some people prefer to have clear work and home hours. Others prefer the lines between home and work to be more blurred. If that's the case, you might slip out to the gym in the middle of the day, but will be on your laptop and working after your kids go to bed. These boundaries aren't right or wrong, just different. The challenges arise when there isn't an alignment between the person's preference and the job, or when managers impose their style on you. When it comes to sexual harassment, people have different preferences around how they like to be greeted, what they expect as physical, nonsexual touch, and the kinds of jokes they find both funny and appropriate for work.

Both individual and organizational practices around boundaries are critical to a safe working environment, but can be uncomfortable to discuss without practice. The next two practice conversations are designed to illuminate the ways in which power and boundary-setting affect your relationships and organizational culture.

PRACTICE CONVERSATION #4

DISPLAY OF AFFECTION

The degree to which employees are touched—and bothered by it—varies across individuals and teams, and can be culturally informed. By working through a scenario about unwanted displays of affection, you create an opportunity to speak about preferences around hugs, handshakes, and touch; practice language around setting and respecting boundaries; practice skills and language around bystander intervention; and consider the impact of unwanted touch in workplace relationships.

> Conversation Starter: *Natalie and Raj are meeting with Richard for the first time. Richard reaches out to shake Raj's hand and then leans in to kiss Natalie on the cheek. How should Natalie respond? How should Raj respond?*

Possible Responses

- Natalie should set a boundary with Richard, in the moment or after the fact.

- Richard shouldn't kiss Natalie.

- Raj should intervene, in the moment or after the fact.

Display of Affection—1

- Nothing needs to happen—this interaction is entirely appropriate.

Reflection and Discussion Questions

- What might Natalie say in this situation? What would affect her ability to say it?

- If Natalie doesn't want to be kissed, what skills or support might she need to address this behavior? Why might this interaction be annoying or unsafe for Natalie?

- What might Raj say or do in the moment? What would affect his ability to do or say what you suggest?

- How might Raj, Natalie, or Richard's relative power (gender, position, cultural background) improve or impede their ability or likelihood to respond in a particular way?

- How might a whole-picture perspective impact an interpretation or response to this scenario?

- What conversations between Raj and Natalie might have happened in advance of this situation that could inform your response?

- If the kiss was unwanted, who might be in a position to talk to Richard? What would they say?

Benefits of Conversation

- Articulate your preferences around touch and greetings and understand how they differ from others on your team or in your organization.

- Build skills at boundary-setting, respecting boundaries, and asking questions about boundaries—in advance of interactions.

- Gain insight into how gender and culture may impact our approach to physical touch.

PRACTICE CONVERSATION #5

UNCLEAR BOUNDARIES AND COMMUNICATION

While some behaviors or actions are clearly in the wrong, other situations are, on the surface, murky. In many cases, context does matter and more information is required. This scenario is deliberately vague. It offers you a chance to explore how your own orientation toward boundaries might influence your response to this and similar scenarios.

> Conversation Starter: *Mike asks Michelle to join him for a drink after work. Michelle politely declines, and then Mike asks her again the following week. After the third time, Michelle starts feeling really uncomfortable and lets her manager know about it. What should the manager do?*

Possible Responses

- The manager/HR should take action.
  Mike is engaging in predatory, stalking behavior.

- The manager/HR should do nothing.
  Michelle is overreacting.

- The manager/HR should investigate.
  It's unclear what's actually happening.

Reflection and Discussion Questions

- How can managers and colleagues respond when an incident is unclear? As their manager, what follow-up questions might you have for Mike or Michelle? How might Mike or Michelle respond to those questions?

- What is the impact of this situation on Michelle? What is the impact of this situation on Mike?

- How might additional context or information about Mike or Michelle inform your responses? For example, what if Mike repeatedly invites colleagues out for drinks after they say no? What if Michelle had been stalked in college? How might this influence her reaction to Mike's invitation?

- Why might it be important to understand more about the interaction between Mike and Michelle? Play out your responses to the above questions based on the following two possibilities:

  — Michelle told Mike initially that she had plans versus saying, "No thank you, I'm not interested in having drinks with you."

  — Mike asked Michelle out for a "cozy drink at my favorite bar" versus what turned out to be a weekly group outing.

- How might Michelle have set a boundary in this situation? How might Mike have missed the boundary or chosen to ignore it?

Benefits of Conversation

- Provides opportunities to reflect on how human resources investigations or manager conversations about harassment may reveal additional context influencing decisions about next steps.

- Highlights ways that ineffective communication can lead to people feeling unsafe.

- Permits practicing language around boundary-setting in a low-stakes context, and illustrates different approaches for setting boundaries.

CHAPTER SUMMARY

▶ Power dynamics impact the way we engage in conversations about boundaries, behavior, and relationships at work. These dynamics also affect how our words are heard and interpreted.

▶ Boundaries are sometimes hard to set and hard to respect. When it comes to workplace boundaries, we need to understand our own style and the style of our colleagues to navigate important conversations about preferences.

▶ Practice Conversations #3, #4, and #5 offer opportunities to explore our styles around boundary-setting, our ability to recognize boundaries, and how boundaries impact safety and respect at work.

CHAPTER 11

RESPONDING TO DISCLOSURES AND SUPPORTING SURVIVORS

RESPONDING TO A REPORT OF SEXUAL HARASSMENT OR ASSAULT

Whether or not you are a manager, at some point in your professional career you will likely have someone share with you a personal experience of sexual harassment at work, or of sexual abuse or assault that happened at some other point in their life. These disclosures are important moments, both for the individual disclosing the experience and, in the case of sexual harassment, for the organization.

If you've found yourself fumbling for the right words to say in this situation, you aren't alone. Handling a disclosure of sexual harassment or assault is absolutely an uncomfortable conversation. As a manager or colleague, it's hard to hear that someone has been harmed or frightened on your watch, and frequently you will also know the person who is being accused of the inappropriate behavior.

For organizations, a mishandled report can create a complicated mess. If managers don't recognize sexual harassment as such, they may fail to notify the appropriate parties and miss a serial perpetrator. A positive reporting experience can go a long way toward building trust in the culture, the process, and the leadership's commitment to employee safety. Managers are typically eager for this kind of training.

These are uncomfortable conversations you can practice. And they are worth practicing, because you can't grab your manual once that office door closes and the words start spilling out of your colleague's mouth.

It's possible to approach disclosures using a lens of compliance, uncomfortable conversations, and empathy together. Whether you're handling a disclosure of sexual harassment as a manager, or responding to a colleague sharing a personal history of sexual abuse or assault outside of work, you should use these four steps.

1. BELIEVE THE PERSON WAS IMPACTED. Recognize the report as a report, and take it at face value. While, in a legal sense, you may not be able to verify facts presented to you in the conversation, you can still believe that the person was impacted and respond accordingly. It takes an incredible amount of courage and grit to disclose sexual harassment or assault. Speaking up comes with risks—personal, social, and professional.

Even if you don't actually believe the person, have questions about what they are telling you, or are required as a part of your role to conduct a formal investigation, a disclosure conversation is not necessarily the time to pursue this line of inquiry. This person trusted you enough to share something unsettling or scary. Respond in kind. If you're hearing about a workplace incident, you may know both parties involved. It may be surprising or unsurprising that a colleague is being accused. You can express empathy in an initial disclosure conversation and still conduct a fair and thorough investigation.

If you'd like a script to use, here are some response options.

- Thank you for sharing that with me.

- I'm sure it took a lot of courage to share that.

- I appreciate you trusting me with this information.

- I can see this really had an impact on you.

In the case of a personal disclosure of previous sexual abuse or assault, you'll want to first establish whether the person is feeling physically and psychologically safe. A simple question like "Have you been able to find the help and support you need?" can usually give you insights into whether the person is on a healing pathway or looking for support in finding one by talking to you.

2. EXPRESS EMPATHY. Empathy is about centering your response on another person's feelings. It's not your job to fix the situation. Your role right now is to be an active listener and accept whatever feelings or reactions are being expressed.

Empathy is not interrogation. It's not asking a million questions or "getting to the bottom" of the story. Let the person take the lead on how much they want to share or disclose. Even if eventually you will be the person who will have to ask some follow-up questions about an incident of harassment to better understand what happened, you don't always need to do that in the first conversation.

Judging or questioning someone's reaction is not empathy. People respond to being sexually harassed or assaulted in lots of different ways. While some survivors might be really angry, others might seem resigned or numb. Some people might be crying, while others might want to hit the gym or drink a bottle of wine. Any of these responses to unsettling and upsetting events is normal.

In the case of workplace sexual harassment, you may be talking to someone who has been sexually victimized at a previous point in their life. Previous experiences can color someone's reactions to today's experiences, so while an incident may feel minor to you, it might not feel minor to someone else.

Stay focused on what the other person is sharing and how they are feeling. You will have time to unpack your responses after the conversation is over, and it's best not to do that with the person who disclosed to you.

If you'd like a script, here are some options.

- It makes sense to me that you would feel . . .

- This situation really stinks.

- I can imagine it's hard to figure out what to do next.

3. EMPOWER. Empowering someone who has disclosed an incident of workplace sexual harassment means knowing and explaining the options for next steps. While it's tempting to give advice, it's important to let the person who disclosed the incident feel ownership over the next steps to the extent possible, given the situation.

In the context of workplace sexual harassment, the primary options are to formally report or not formally report, speak directly to the person whose behavior or words were harassing, or do nothing. Alongside any of these options, the person can seek outside guidance around next steps or emotional support to help with the impact of harassment. People also have options about timing for next steps or key decisions, such as waiting an hour, a day, or a week before choosing any of the options described above.

For managers required to report incidents to human resources or for human resources professionals themselves, the options can be more limited, but you still have some to choose from. Ideally, the person disclosing an incident of workplace harassment knows that the conversation with a manager is an official report and has chosen that option on purpose. Ask the person how they would like to proceed: Do you want to report this up the chain immediately, or schedule a time to do it in the future (obviously, within reason)?

Is there a particular member of the human resources team with whom you feel most comfortable? Do you want to reach out directly or do you want me to reach out? Do you want to call, email, or see them in person?

4. KEEP BUILDING YOUR KNOWLEDGE. You will be more likely to believe someone if you know what sexual harassment looks like and how it plays out in your organization. You will believe people of all genders if you understand that sexual harassment is about power, not gender. You will be better able to empower people if you have knowledge of the options available to them in various situations. When someone starts sharing a story or incident, that's not the time to be researching options online or finding your flowchart about reporting options.

Disclosing an incident of sexual harassment can, of course, be difficult and challenging for the person making the disclosure. That's why it's important for others on a team or in an organization to be prepared to handle the topic. Responding to a disclosure is a specific kind of uncomfortable conversation—when viewed through the eyes of the person receiving the disclosure—and is worth practicing in a low-stakes environment. It's also a skill that translates outside of the workplace, and can be helpful with friends or loved ones who have experienced or may experience sexual abuse, assault, or harassment.

ONE FINAL TIP. Don't forget to take care of yourself! Whether you are experienced at hearing disclosures of sexual harassment or violence or it's your first conversation, it's emotionally draining work and can bring up a lot of different emotions. Debriefing a conversation in a confidential context with someone other than the person who experienced harassment or violence is a useful way of processing your approach as well as your feelings.

BEFORE YOU GET STARTED:
KEY ISSUES IMPACTING DISCLOSURES AND REPORTS

While practice conversations will inevitably bring up questions and clarifications, a few key areas are worth understanding if your role requires you to formally handle complaints of sexual harassment.

- **REPORTING PROCESS.** How are reports of sexual harassment handled within your organization? Who receives the report? What is the investigation process? By asking these questions up front, you can begin to imagine how you might respond if an incident of sexual harassment takes place.

- **MANDATED OR OBLIGATED REPORTING.** Some organizations require managers to report any reported or witnessed incident of harassment through a central human resources or legal officer. Others apply this standard only to employees who are directly managed. If your company has a mandated reporting policy, it impacts how you might respond to witnessing troubling behavior and requires you to think through how to support colleagues who may experience sexual harassment but don't want to report it.

- **ANONYMOUS REPORTING.** Tools are now available to support anonymous reporting of sexual harassment, and some companies are putting them to use to encourage reporting of unwanted or troubling behavior. Anonymous reporting can be a good way to check the pulse on types of complaints or behaviors that may present training opportunities. You may want to ask some questions about how anonymous reporting is handled. How are these reports investigated? Will the victim be outed? What information gets reported? Is it actionable?

PRACTICE CONVERSATION #6

OBSTACLES TO REPORTING

There are real reasons why sexual harassment isn't reported, including a fear of not being believed, inaction, overly severe action, or professional consequences. At the same time, companies cannot address sexual harassment effectively unless it is reported. Practicing uncomfortable conversations around a scenario that reveals this tension helps companies understand obstacles to reporting and helps employees explore how this tension plays out.

Conversation Starter: *One night, Marquis and Jada, two peers in the same department, go out for a drink after work. After a few drinks, Jada confesses that an executive in the organization (her boss's boss), Desiree, has been pressuring her to go on a date. At first it seemed like she was joking, but now she's not sure how to say no. She really likes her job, and doesn't want to report it. The next day, Marquis checks in, and Jada seems panicked that she confessed this. She really doesn't want to make a big deal out of it and asks Marquis to keep it a secret. How should Marquis handle this situation?*

Possible Responses

- Marquis should keep Jada's confession a secret.

- Marquis should report Jada's situation.

- Marquis should try to convince Jada to report this incident.

Discussion and Reflection Questions

- Why might Marquis keep Jada's confession a secret? What would the impact be on Jada? What would the impact be on Marquis? What would the impact be on the organization?

- Why might Marquis report this incident? Whom would he report it to? What would he say? How would he communicate this decision to Jada? What would the impact of reporting it be on Jada?

- What if Marquis knew, confidentially, that Desiree was engaging in the same behavior with another employee?

How might this change his response (and/or Jada's reaction to it)?

- What does "convincing" Jada look like? Are there ways to support or empower her without convincing her?

- What information might Jada and/or Marquis need to have in order to make an informed decision about what to do next? For example, does Marquis know what the reporting options are within the company? Does Marquis know about resources that might provide Jada with support in this situation? Might human resources have relevant information? Is there a way for Marquis or Jada to report this anonymously to human resources? How might Jada and/or Marquis go about getting this information? How might missing information have been helpful to inform this scenario or the possible responses to it?

- What additional conversations might Jada and Marquis have with each other about this conversation? Why might timing be important? Is there anyone else, not described in the scenario, who might play a role in supporting Jada?

As in the case with other practice conversations, take some time to reflect on and share the "why" behind your response; be as specific as possible when you suggest possible responses for either Jada or Marquis.

Benefits of Conversation

- Offers opportunities to understand obstacles to reporting.

- Practices using empowering thinking and language in response to those who have experienced harassment.

- Provides colleagues an opportunity to reflect on what information they want to know or consider in advance of disclosing an incident or hearing about one in the organization.

- Builds awareness about the role of human resources in addressing harassment.

- **RELEVANT LEGAL ISSUES.** The legal climate on sexual harassment is changing rapidly, so it's important to stay apprised and review policy on an annual basis and have materials on hand before you dive into practice conversations.

- **THIRD-PARTY HARASSMENT.** Third-party harassment is harassment committed by someone who is not a company employee, like a sales prospect, vendor, customer, or investor. You will want to understand whether your company has a policy around third-party harassment, and how to handle reports of incidents that may be most relevant to your work or the work of your team.

- **ROLE OF HUMAN RESOURCES.** In most organizations, someone from human resources will conduct the investigation of a reported incident of harassment, determine an outcome, and implement consequences. While human resource professionals can be—and usually are—empathetic human beings, they are not the same as professional counselors or advocates—and they are often required to play a formal role when it comes to handling sexual harassment complaints that may impact their ability to provide emotional support.

CASE STUDY **MY COLLEAGUE WAS ASSAULTED AND NEEDS SUPPORT**

Let's review one more case study. Here's one we did in a workshop with a group of sales managers.

> One night, after a glass of wine, Amy's colleague Avery confesses that one of her sales prospects made an aggressive pass at her earlier that week. Amy and Avery work on the sales team together, reporting to the same manager. The incident scared Avery pretty badly, but she doesn't want to tell

CASE STUDY, *cont.*

> *their manager about it. How should Amy advise and*
> *support Avery? What else can Amy do?*

This scenario sparks several areas of discomfort, including how to respond to a friend in an emotional crisis and how to balance obligations to a friend with obligations to your place of employment.

Some possible responses are

- Amy should emotionally support Avery.

- Amy should advise Avery to report the incident internally.

- Amy should advise Avery to NOT report the incident internally.

- Amy should report the incident herself.

- Amy should make an anonymous report, if that's an option.

First and foremost, the group of managers practiced varying ways of expressing empathy toward what Avery experienced. Some managers had more experience in their personal lives responding to friends who had been assaulted, and brought this language to the forefront. Those who were less experienced benefited from hearing different styles of reflective listening and normalizing various responses to an attempted assault.

Then the group spent some time on discussing next steps and options for Avery. A few managers wanted to immediately confront the sales prospect, and, while this was a well-intentioned instinct, it wasn't expressed in the most empowering ways. Instead, we talked about how to make an initial disclosure conversation centered on Avery and what Avery wants, even if it's not our personal first instinct. Several people also pointed out places to use the word "could" instead of "should" when discussing options of what to do next.

CASE STUDY, *cont.*

Additionally, this particular organization was in the process of rolling out a mandated reporting policy, requiring all manager-level employees to formally report incidents of sexual harassment from any person in the organization, not just direct reports. This new policy quickly emerged as a central point in the discussion, as the sales managers grappled with the conflict between their obligation to report and their friend's desire to keep it confidential.

By exploring Amy's discomfort facing a moral dilemma—respecting her friend's wishes versus following policy—we were able to brainstorm ideas about how that dilemma could be avoided. In this scenario, most of the managers assumed that Avery did not know about the policy, and that she might have reconsidered sharing the incident had she known about it. This assumption underlined the importance of proactively and frequently reminding all employees about the new mandated reporting policy, so that no one would be taken by surprise in the moment. The whole picture, in this case, went beyond the conversation about the incident and reflected the types of conversations Amy and Avery had on a regular basis.

Several of the managers dove deep into how they might be able to follow the letter of the policy while still respecting the spirit of Avery's request. For example, could they report the incident anonymously? Could they leave a note? Could they do it in a way that wouldn't come back to Avery? The human resources team, who were present at the training, had to clarify key aspects of the policy for the group and, in some cases, take questions back for review.

The discussion about the new policy sparked a question about where employees could go for support, if not to work colleagues who are managers. By brainstorming together, some of the managers pointed to the importance of professional groups and mentors outside of the organization. A few employees also mentioned outside resources, online or in-

CASE STUDY, *cont.*

person, that specialize in supporting people who experience sexual harassment or assault.

At the core of this scenario is the question of why Avery might hesitate to report an incident to her own manager. The group speculated on why this might be the case, and generated a solid list of reasons, ranging from losing a performance incentive, fear of inaction or not being believed, feeling powerless or overwhelmed, and not understanding or trusting the process. For each reason, I followed up with a question about the conversations that could happen today that might address or tackle that reason. What would she need to know in order to feel confident about reporting?

One woman's response led to an important discussion about the tensions that exist in organizations around reporting. While there are real reasons why an employee might not want to report an incident like this, organizations cannot hold perpetrators accountable for sexual harassment unless they know that harassment takes place. Furthermore, the effects of this incident go well beyond Avery, especially if this prospect becomes a customer who then interacts with others at the organization. This part of the whole picture was important to explore and understand.

As with the other scenarios and conversations in this book, this practice conversation provided insights on policy, built skills for handling disclosures in compliant and empathetic ways, and illuminated potential obstacles to reporting harassment at this particular organization.

By using this practice conversation approach, every person has the chance to practice uncomfortable conversations, hear how others approach uncomfortable conversations, and reflect on the skills they have or could use to approach similar conversations in the future. These practice conversations are the process by which individuals and organizations develop the skills necessary to prevent and respond to sexual harassment.

UNDERSTANDING THE IMPACT OF SEXUAL ABUSE
AND ASSAULT ON THE WORKPLACE

Every day, survivors of sexual abuse and assault go to work. As mentioned earlier, in the United States, one in three women[1] and one in six men[2] have reported some form of sexual violence. The rate of sexual violence skyrockets when individuals are transgender, affecting one out of every two.[3] Yet few workplaces acknowledge how the experiences of these survivors affect how they work in both negative and positive ways.

It's first worth noting that surviving sexual abuse and assault, especially when an individual is provided with access to help and healing, can result in the development of numerous traits and skills that bring huge benefits to workplaces. For example, my ability to manage others, handle the most challenging of external clients, or understand the world through the eyes of someone else comes directly from the skills I learned through healing. When we are able to acknowledge the experience of sexual abuse or assault in the workplace through uncomfortable conversations, we're better able to understand and access those skills and leverage them within our organization.

At the same time, surviving sexual abuse or assault may also result in someone feeling less safe among people who share characteristics with a perpetrator or feeling alarmed by certain behaviors, like an unexpected hand on the shoulder or unwanted hugs. By considering the experience of survivors through practice conversations, it's possible to bring these potential hot spots to the surface without asking survivors to self-disclose. The experience of survivors of previous sexual trauma is a key part of the whole-picture perspective when it comes to uncomfortable conversations.

Keeping a traumatic history to yourself—whether it's because you view it as private or fear the response of your colleagues—requires emotional and mental energy. When people who have not directly experienced sexual abuse or assault can acknowledge and honor these experiences in the workplace, it takes the onus off survivors. It's powerful to hear a leader, manager, or other person in power acknowledge a personal experience. It builds trust that the organization can handle difficult, uncomfortable topics, like reports of sexual harassment or misconduct.

By understanding the experiences of these survivors better, organizations can design more inclusive spaces and teams in the workplace. This also adds to psychological safety and productivity—the central goals of an effective approach to sexual harassment prevention and response. On this topic, some pertinent questions to ask include

- Where can employees get mental health support during a crisis?

- What physical spaces help people feel safe enough to work?

- Do your travel policies take into consideration safety concerns for solo travelers?

- Are employees required to travel or attend meetings alone? What are the mechanisms you have in place to ensure that those employees feel—and are—safe?

The degree to which your workplace is able to accommodate the experience and perspective of those who have been sexually assaulted or abused will directly impact its ability to prevent and respond to sexual harassment. When we show support for survivors, we signal that our workplace is prepared to handle other kinds of uncomfortable conversations. Imagine that your company organizes a picnic. Five managers show up. Four of them are wearing shirts reflecting their favorite sports teams. One is wearing a t-shirt from last year's walk to support a local rape crisis center. Knowing nothing else about these managers, which one do you think would be most likely to provide support and empathy around the experience of sexual harassment?

In the final scenario in this chapter, you'll have an opportunity to think about your own empathy toward survivors of sexual violence and reflect on how you can help your organization become more survivor-friendly.

PRACTICE CONVERSATION #7

SURVIVORS AT WORK

A scenario exploring the experience of survivors at work serves several purposes. First, it gives visibility to the experience of survivors who may not feel comfortable sharing their histories. Second, it offers another angle on the importance of bystander intervention, and the reasons why some colleagues might react differently to various uncomfortable conversations.

Conversation Starter: *Last year, Jessica noticed that Maria posted something about a personal experience with sexual assault on Twitter. Maria hasn't brought it up at work, but during a lunchtime conversation about a politician accused of sexually assaulting multiple people, Maria got really quiet and went back to her workstation. What should Jessica say or do next?*

Possible Responses

- Jessica should speak directly to Maria about her experiences with sexual assault.

- Jessica should generally check in with Maria.

- It's okay and good to discuss personal experiences at work.

- It's scary, risky, and inappropriate to raise personal experiences at work.

Survivors at Work—1

Discussion and Reflection Questions

- What might make Maria more or less likely to discuss her personal experience at work? How might other employees feel if Maria spoke openly about her experiences?

- Are there ways Jessica could have talked about this sooner? What, specifically, could she have said? Why might Jessica have chosen to say nothing?

- How can you let someone know you are available if they want to talk, but without forcing the issue? What are some strategies for dropping clues that you might be friendly on this issue if someone wanted to talk about it?

- How might employees know who has experience and interest in being a support person in the workplace around sexual assault and abuse that isn't work-related?

- Are there ways your company can accommodate survivors (or allies of survivors) for whom certain conversations or topics may evoke strong emotions? How does the company encourage employees to care for themselves in this way?

Take a moment to reflect back on some of the other scenarios presented earlier. How might your responses shift if you knew that one or more person involved in the incident was a survivor of sexual abuse or assault?

Benefits of Conversation

- Indirectly communicates support to survivors of sexual abuse and assault.

- Breaks the ice on ways organizations or teams can provide further support to survivors.

- Reveals how these conversations might support trauma survivors.

CHAPTER SUMMARY

▸ Responding to a disclosure of sexual harassment is a required skill for managers at most companies, and one of the most important conversations to practice in advance of a real-life scenario.

▸ By practicing a disclosure conversation using Practice Conversation #6, you can try out language that both meets the compliance requirements of your company and is empathetic to those who have been affected by an interaction at work or by a previous trauma.

▸ All of us work with survivors of sexual abuse or assault, whether we know it directly or not. When we create workplaces that consider their experiences, we make the workplace safer and more inclusive for all who experienced trauma and send a much-needed message that sexual violence is unacceptable to our workplace and community.

CHAPTER 12

PRACTICE AND HABITS

HOW TO KEEP THE CONVERSATIONS GOING

Uncomfortable conversations are both a skill and a habit. While a running skills clinic can show you that running a few miles is possible, it requires more than a one-day event to turn you from a couch potato into a daily runner. That's why it's important to create an extended training plan for your uncomfortable conversations. Similar to running, getting off the couch is the hardest part. Once you are laced up and out the door, you can put one foot in front of the other for thirty minutes, and will be more likely to do it on a regular basis.

By dedicating time to conversations about sexual harassment prevention and response, you demonstrate your commitment to creating a safer and more inclusive environment. More important, you can carve out a habit of incorporating topics that are typically avoided in the workplace. First conversations are the hardest. The sooner you or your team gets them out of the way, the sooner new habits begin to form.

NINE-WEEK MANAGER-LED CONVERSATION PLAN

Leaders can use the following guide to structure a series of meetings with those who report to them. Before and after each of these meetings, it is very useful for the leader to conduct at least a few one-on-one conversations with selected participants and to make it clear to all participants that they are invited to initiate that kind of private conversation as well. The leader should use these conversations to gather feedback, discuss things participants are reluctant to raise in the group, and check to see if anyone is managing a strong reaction in response to any of the discussions.

The leader might also designate a participant (preferably of another gender) to assist in conducting these individual conversations. The leader and anyone assisting the leader can then collaborate on using the information gathered in those conversations in planning for subsequent meetings. The content of those one-on-one meetings should be considered confidential, unless the two people in the meeting agree otherwise.

SAMPLE NINE-WEEK MANAGER-LED CONVERSATION PLAN

Week 1 **Policy and Process**

- Pre-Reading: Start Here: Why We Need More Uncomfortable Conversations at Work and Chapter 1

- Review company policies on sexual harassment. If your organization utilizes an online training or annual in-person training, use or review the material.

- Review your company's flowchart for reporting incidents of sexual harassment, reflecting both internal resources and resources in the community. If your company doesn't have one, create one.

- Consider inviting your assigned human resources representative or the person in your organization most knowledgeable about compliance to join your team meeting.

Discussion Questions

- What questions or comments do participants have about the organization's policies?

- Which reporting pathway might they choose? What are the characteristics of a manager ideally suited to effectively handle a report of harassment?

Week 2 **The Uncomfortable Conversation Framework**

- Pre-Reading: Chapters 2 to 7

- Optional Pre-Work: Ask individual team members to reflect on conversation experience in Chapter 2 or conduct anonymous survey from Chapter 2 to gain insight into experience on your team.

- Review the five elements of the Framework and set up the next several weeks of application of the Framework through practice conversations.

- Remind people about self-care practices: take space, seek outside support if you need it, and provide hotline numbers or local resources for survivors of abuse or assault.

Discussion Questions

- Invite team members to share their reflections following the conversation experience assessment. How might different levels of experience affect the kinds of conversations they have about sexual harassment and violence at work?

- What was surprising or new about
  The Uncomfortable Conversation Framework?
  What resonated with you the most?

Week 3   **Helpful Intervention**

- Pre-Reading: Chapters 8 and 9

- Review "Tips for Effective Intervention"
  in Chapter 9.

- Present Practice Conversations #1 and #2 through
  a think-pair-share exercise. (Reflect on questions
  individually, discuss with one to two peers, and share
  highlights of discussion with the whole group.)

Discussion Questions

- Use discussion and reflection questions from
  Practice Conversations to guide conversation.

Week 4   **Power and Boundaries**

- Pre-Reading: Chapter 10

- Review "Recognizing and Addressing Power"
  in Chapter 10.

- Present Practice Conversations #3, #4, and #5
  through a think-pair-share exercise (see Week 3).

Discussion Questions

- Ask team members to share how power shows up
  in their workplace relationships and interactions.

- Use discussion and reflection questions from
  Practice Conversations to guide conversation.

Week 5 **Responding to Sexual Harassment and Violence**

- Pre-Reading: Chapter 11

- Present Practice Conversations #6 and #7 through a think-pair-share exercise (see Week 3).

- Consider inviting your HR representative, depending on your experience level handling reports through a compliance lens.

Discussion Questions

- Revisit policies and reporting practices in light of the group's discussion of Chapter 11.

- Use discussion and reflection questions from Practice Conversations to guide conversation.

Week 6 **Sexual Assault Awareness Initiative**

- Announce your participation in a national awareness initiative related to sexual abuse or assault, even though that initiative may involve events in the future.

- Seek volunteers for a committee to help organize participation.

Discussion Questions

- Are there other ways that you, as a manager, can proactively show support for survivors of sexual abuse or assault? Do members of your team have some quick wins that you might try out?

Week 7 **Crowd-Source Practice Conversations**

- Prior to the meeting, send out a brief, anonymous survey asking for topics that could be workshopped through scenarios.

Discussion Questions

- Discuss the results as a group, and prioritize several additional practice conversations for future meetings.

- If time permits, begin working on one of the scenarios immediately.

Week 8 **Custom Practice Conversations**

- Present a scenario developed as a part of last week's group discussion and reflect on possible responses.

Week 9 **Skills Development**

- Based on the skills discussed and addressed in previous sessions, pick a topic where you can invite an expert or hire a trainer: bystander intervention, implicit bias/power dynamics, conflict management, feedback, or handling a disclosure of harassment or assault or any other situation deemed relevant.

- If you don't have the resources for training, consider reading two to three articles on the topic and discussing them as a group or continuing with practice conversations on a monthly basis.

HABITS FOR MANAGERS

By incorporating opportunities for conversation into all-staff meetings, team meetings, and individual one-on-one meetings with managers, you can begin to build a culture of uncomfortable conversation that will result in improved behavior and relationships in a gender-diverse workplace. The key is to make uncomfortable conversations—specifically on the topic of sexual harassment and misconduct—a regular part of your workplace.

By initiating the nine-week training program, you will develop a set of customized practice conversations to guide future conversations and gain insight into which skills your team members may need further training on in order to develop. As you move out of a formal training program, look for ways to keep the conversation going through regular team communications and meetings.

Consider the following ideas to get you started:

- Create a weekly email series following the uncomfortable conversation kickoff, which can be repeated once a year as a part of Sexual Assault Awareness Month.

- Workshop a scenario or practice conversation from your list of scenarios.

- Build a standing agenda item into your meeting that addresses workplace behavior and relationships.

- Add a section to an internal newsletter or communication that highlights uncomfortable conversations at work.

- Request that professional development programs on other topics incorporate a specific example related to sexual harassment or misconduct.

- Rotate an assigned team member to "bring up the uncomfortable conversation" in your everyday work.

- Partner with a local nonprofit organization focused on sexual assault or abuse prevention to keep the topic alive within your team or organization.

- Participate in a national sexual assault awareness day as a team or organization.

- Post resources related to sexual harassment prevention and response in public or shared spaces.

- Form a working group to highlight ways in which your organization could be friendlier to survivors of sexual abuse or assault.

- Repeat the nine-week training on an annual basis, especially as your team adds new members.

ACTION STEPS FOR INDIVIDUALS

You don't need a formal group or internal training program to keep this work going on your own. As an employee, you can initiate conversations about sexual harassment and violence in your role. The more you do this and engage others, the more you will break the habit of silence within your team and organization. You don't need to wait for your manager or CEO to start this work; in fact, your actions and the conversations you initiate can help lead to organization-wide changes.

The following is a list of possible actions. You may think of others to add. Please do not try to do all of them at once. Spreading these actions out over a period of weeks or even months may have an even greater impact. And by taking action, you may find others who wish to do so as well.

I. **KNOW THE FACTS ABOUT POLICY.** Ask your manager for a copy of your organization's sexual harassment policy and ask how reports are handled. You signal to both your manager and your human resources department that you are paying attention to both policy and process.

2. **START THE CONVERSATION WITH COLLEAGUES.** Ask a colleague whom they might talk to if they experienced sexual harassment in the workplace and share your own response with them. You will help someone else in your organization think through a future uncomfortable conversation.

3. **SHOW SUPPORT FOR SURVIVORS OF ABUSE AND ASSAULT.** Find a local organization that helps people who have experienced sexual abuse or assault. Invite your colleagues to volunteer or donate. You signal to colleagues that you are someone who would potentially be supportive to survivors. This helps take pressure off survivors to self-identify if that doesn't make sense for them.

4. **BUILD SKILLS.** Ask your manager if you can participate in a bystander intervention training. Explain what bystander intervention is and why it's important for your role. Even if your manager chooses not to invest in this training, you have started a conversation about the topic and its role in safe and productive workplaces.

5. **GO FOR A QUICK WIN.** Post a number for a sexual assault hotline in a place where your colleagues will see it. You can help others start conversations simply by posting something as simple as a hotline number.

6. **ENCOURAGE MORE CONVERSATION.** Share a relevant article or blog post about sexual harassment prevention and response with your team. You may be met with silence, or you may find others who want to join you in your journey of uncomfortable conversations.

START AN UNCOMFORTABLE CONVERSATION GROUP

If you are passionate about this approach and in a position to self-organize within your company or industry, you might want to consider establishing a formal uncomfortable conversation group. The purpose of a group like this is to become embedded "conversation starters" within your organization, and establish yourselves as a set of colleagues capable of handling uncomfortable conversations about sexual harassment and misconduct.

Implementing an uncomfortable conversation group at your company is an easy way to build individual skills in uncomfortable conversations and to use those skills to prevent sexual harassment from taking place. Even a small group of employees can play an important role in changing the culture and climate.

It is worth noting here that what I am suggesting is not something like a solidarity and support group. Such groups have their place and can be powerful in their own ways, but in order to practice uncomfortable conversations, the goal must be just that—to practice uncomfortable conversations. A group that is solely composed of women or survivors speaking about the direct experience of sexual harassment should be carried out in another context, ideally one with some level of professional therapy or psychological support and HR oversight. An uncomfortable conversation group is designed to be a diverse group of employees who can provide insight into responding to a disclosure, brainstorm ways to appropriately intervene, and reflect on how to take accountability and learn from mistakes.

Once you assemble a group and begin to meet regularly, consistently invite new colleagues to join. By developing a strong drop-in culture, you can encourage others to use the group to workshop their own uncomfortable conversations with you.

Your first several meetings will follow the steps outlined in the

Nine-Week Manager-Led Conversation Plan, which will walk you through the steps of a skills-based approach to preventing and responding to sexual harassment and provide some initial opportunities to practice. Once the group is grounded in these initial steps and has built some practice time together, the rest of your time can focus on the following themes:

- Where is our organization avoiding conversations about sexual harassment and violence? How can we, given our roles and responsibilities, break the ice on this topic and get more conversations going?

- How can we let our colleagues know that we are willing to enter uncomfortable conversations? How do we "market" our group both to the people who may have experienced harassment, abuse, or assault and to those who may be questioning their own behavior and attitudes?

- What additional skills do we, as a group, need if we're going to facilitate uncomfortable conversations more effectively? How can we help develop those skills? (Some ideas for deep-dive skills that help support good facilitation are public speaking, media training, conflict management, giving and receiving feedback, and bystander intervention.)

- How can our company become more responsive and sensitive to the survivors of sexual abuse and assault who work here? Can we engage others around some of these activities, such as participating in sexual assault awareness days or supporting local nonprofits dedicated to sexual abuse or assault prevention?

- How can we advocate for a skills-based approach to sexual harassment prevention and response within our organization?

Develop a timeline and track your progress in building conversation experience and skills within your organization. Whatever your role in the organization, you can help break the habit of silence and establish new habits of conversation.

CHAPTER SUMMARY

▸ To replace a habit of silence with a habit of uncomfortable conversation requires a plan that incorporates intentional practice.

▸ For managers, this means dedicating regular time to training and practice, as outlined in this book. Managers can also support their conversation habits by designing ways to proactively start uncomfortable conversations through standing meetings, manager check-ins, and other structures already in place.

▸ For individual employees, intentional practice means making a commitment to starting conversations with your manager and peers on a regular basis. Individual employees can also support this work by starting an employee group dedicated to starting and sustaining uncomfortable conversations in the workplace.

▸ The more conversations you and your colleagues can initiate within your organization, the better positioned you will be to build skills, change culture, and ultimately break the habit of silence that contributes to unsafe workplaces.

CHAPTER 13

NAVIGATING COMMON CONVERSATION CHALLENGES

While it's impossible to address every possible question or challenge that may arise as organizations dive into conversations about behavior, relationships, and boundaries at work, a few themes are worth addressing specifically. This chapter provides guidance for how to navigate common challenges that come up when rolling out a skills-based approach to sexual harassment prevention and response.

CAN I DATE MY COLLEAGUE?

Does this mean that workplace romances are dead? We spend so much time at work. What if we fall in love? Aren't we consenting adults?

Hmm, but I'm having feelings for a colleague, client, or vendor. Are these feelings wrong? Am I not allowed to act on them?

When we talk about boundaries, behavior, and relationships at work, it's inevitable that romantic relationships will come up in the conversation. After all, people are spending more time at work than ever before, and it can be a way to meet and interact with new people.

While relationships between managers and subordinates are

particularly susceptible to potential abuse of power, many examples exist of consensual, lasting relationships that started when two people worked together at the same organization.

When considering a workplace relationship, it's necessary to consider your organization's policy alongside an analysis of the beginning, middle, and potential end of a relationship—all while feeling romantic feelings toward a new person. Even if there's a policy against such relationships, that policy can't dictate people's feelings, only their behavior.

If you are personally considering or reflecting on a workplace relationship, here are some questions to consider.

- What are the policies about workplace relationships at my organization? Are they communicated frequently and clearly?

- Are the policies consistently enforced? Are relationships or hookups taking place behind closed doors? What is the impact of secrecy on the culture of the organization?

- What will the possible effect of my relationship be on my career? My relationships with my colleagues? My partner's career and relationships?

- Are my feelings going to be passing or lasting? What would happen if I didn't act on these feelings?

Workplace relationships require skill to navigate policies, the potential impact on your professional lives and roles, and consideration of how you will both professionally survive if the relationship doesn't. If you want to explore the realistic potential of a workplace relationship wisely and without facing repercussions at your organization, engage in some uncomfortable conversations with your potential partner and be sure that you fully understand the policies at your organization.

SHOULD I JUST AVOID PEOPLE WHO AREN'T MY GENDER?

*Is it okay to have an after-work drink or private dinner
with a colleague of the opposite gender?*

I'm going to just move into a women-only co-working space.

*Well, I'm just never going to have a solo meeting with a woman
ever again.*

These comments and questions are all common reactions to the
volatile conversations about sexual harassment circling in our
workplaces; they are a natural response to not having the skills to
navigate workplace relationships in light of new awareness about
the prevalence and impact of sexual harassment. But when we
avoid relationships—just as when we avoid conversations—we
aren't solving the challenge at hand. Even worse, we perpetuate
the dynamics that created the volatility in the first place.

Gender separation is usually an attempt to solve a problem
of skill or safety. For example, in the wake of the #MeToo movement, some men avoid women as a way of avoiding accusations of
sexual harassment, and some women seek out women-only spaces
to feel more protected from unwanted comments and behaviors.
In both cases, the gender separation doesn't solve the actual problem—it just avoids the problem altogether.

While there is a time and a place for gender separation, it's
important to be intentional about how to approach it and the effect
it has on your workplace. When you or others in your workplace
share statements like those above, you can use practical questions
to determine the underlying challenge that separation may be trying to solve.

- What would the impact be of avoiding a gender altogether?
  What would be the impact on my professional life? My
  personal life? My values?

- What are you most afraid might happen behind closed doors? What would make you feel confident or safe in a closed-door meeting?

- Are there certain situations where you feel more or less safe with people of a different gender? What makes those situations different?

- How do my moral or religious values affect how I feel about being alone with someone of another gender? How do I negotiate these values in the context of what is fair, right, and acceptable at work?

When you pinpoint the challenge, you can begin to have uncomfortable conversations about it. By pausing the reaction, embracing discomfort, seeing the whole picture, and asking curious questions, it's possible to come up with ideas that will make gender-diverse workplaces safe again.

WHAT IF MY FRIENDS ARE JERKS?

Sometimes these trainings lead people to realize that they have been silent in the face of their friends saying troubling things and behaving in inappropriate ways. This can create a predicament. For instance, a young man, Chris, recently approached me for advice about one of his work friends who was constantly commenting on the appearance of the new class of summer interns, and whether they seemed like suitable dating prospects. Chris was offended by his friend's behavior, and also concerned that being associated with him might make people think he was inappropriate as well. He wanted my advice on how to end the workplace relationship.

Walking away from inappropriate friends is certainly an option, as I told Chris. But of course, I had a few curious questions to add as well. "Have you tried talking to your friend about his behavior?" I asked. "If so, what was his response?"

I saw that Chris didn't want his friend to behave that way. He realized inaction is part of the problem, and he wanted to take action, maybe by walking away from the friendship completely. This is definitely an option, but it's one that continues the habit of avoiding uncomfortable conversations.

Instead, I recommended that Chris consider ways he might use his influence to help engage his friend and those impacted by his behavior in more productive conversations. In the case of his friend, this doesn't mean that Chris has to turn every comment into a serious discussion, but it does mean that he will have to take more risks to get curious about offensive jokes or inappropriate comments when they come up. Perhaps more effectively, he could also bring up the topic in a more general way before a comment is made. Chris could also speak to other peers in his group after his friend makes a comment. Chris might assume that their silence signals agreement with his friend's views, when, in fact, that silence stems from a similar kind of discomfort.

When peers walk away from people whose behavior is troubling or is negatively impacting our workplaces, the people left to lead the uncomfortable conversations are frequently the people who are being most severely affected. In the case of Chris and his friend, if Chris walks away from the friendship, the only people left to have the conversation are the offensive friend, people who tolerate or support the comments, and the interns themselves. If the worst thing that will happen is losing a friendship that you've already decided you're willing to lose, why not use your influence as a peer first? If you aren't going to talk to the person, who will?

Here are some tips for maintaining accountability in conversations with peers:

- Start with care and compassion. You don't want your friends to get into trouble. You want them to have productive relationships at work and succeed on the job.

- Stay curious. Consider why they are behaving the way they do. How did they learn to think this behavior was okay? What are they trying to achieve with those comments?

- Don't underestimate the power of peers. When members of a peer group are silent in the face of an inappropriate comment, it's easy to conclude that silence signals agreement. This isn't always the case. Sometimes, when one person has the courage to speak up, other members of the group will find their voices as well.

- You don't have to call out behavior 100 percent of the time to be effective. In fact, always policing people makes you less effective as a support.

- You can be funny sometimes. Sometimes using humor to disrupt and disarm can be an effective tactic for bystander intervention.

HOW DO I ASSESS MY OWN BEHAVIOR?

After this training, I'm now rethinking all of my behavior and conversations for the last decade. I'm scared to talk about it or ask questions. How do I know whether I'm behaving appropriately? What do I do if I'm not?

I feel horrible that my behavior might have made other people uncomfortable, or even unsafe. What do I do now? Should I make amends?

If you find yourself personally grappling with these kinds of questions, consider these practical next steps.

The approach that people use when recovering from an addiction through a 12-step process is really helpful. Recall a particular incident where you think you may have behaved inappropriately. Write it down. Think of any other incidents that might be in the same or similar categories. Write those down. Think about whether there are other categories you want to include. This will help you recognize any patterns in your behavior, particular dynamics that you aren't equipped to handle, or situations that are likely to trigger an inappropriate reaction (for example, alcohol, rejection, certain peers).

Once you've created a list of specific incidents, consider the following questions. Most people answer these questions with a particular incident or group of incidents in mind.

- Is this a pattern of behavior or a one-time incident? For example, did I once make a comment about a colleague's looks or body, or do I regularly engage in conversations with colleagues about which assistant I want to have sex with?

- What information have I learned that is making me reconsider my behavior or actions? What impact is my behavior having on others? On myself? Am I afraid of being fired? Am I discouraged that I'm not living up to my potential? Am I lonely or ashamed?

- What situations are most likely to trigger inappropriate behavior (rejection, a boundary, etc.)? What skills am I lacking?

- What external influences encourage my behavior? Peers? Alcohol? When am I most likely to engage in unhealthy or inappropriate behavior?

- What's my motivation to change? Am I willing to do the work? What might it be like to hear feedback about my behavior and its effects? Am I prepared to take ownership and accountability?

- Who are the people in my life who provide me with support and encouragement when it comes to positive, personal change?

Once you have completed a self-assessment, consider what kind of support you might need to further understand yourself or your behavior. Is this something you can discuss with a trusted friend? Do you need professional support to really make a change? Whatever you decide, take the first step. Throughout the process of change, have some compassion for yourself. You learned unhealthy behaviors over a period of years and it will take time and effort to unlearn them.

I'VE BEEN HARASSED. WHAT DO I DO?

While this book is not a comprehensive guide to responding to the lived experience of sexual harassment, I do want to close with a basic outline of options. First and foremost, if you are harassed—or assaulted—at work, it's not your fault. Whether you freeze, get angry, feel scared, or just don't know what to do, your response is normal. In addition to the options below, please know that you deserve help and support, and there are many free options available by phone, in person, or by text.

Consider the following options in response to sexual harassment:

- Report the incident immediately to a manager or human resources representative, ideally someone you trust.

- Report the incident anonymously, if that's an option at your company.

- Discuss the incident with a trusted colleague, probably a peer, to better understand what happened, its impact, and your options.

- Discuss the incident with an outside expert, friend, or support organization to better understand what happened, its impact, and your options.

- Report the incident externally by filing a complaint with the EEOC, a private attorney, local authorities, or the media.

In all cases, most sexual harassment experts and lawyers recommend documenting the incident immediately. If you are affected emotionally, please seek help and support. Remember, what you do in response to sexual harassment is your choice. No choice is perfect, but all of them are yours.

CHAPTER SUMMARY

- When advising someone about inappropriate behavior, take inventory, use caution when considering amends, and practice compassion.

- Workplace dating and relationships require a higher level of uncomfortable conversation experience and consideration of policy, and are worth addressing as part of a skills-based approach to sexual harassment prevention and response.

- If the topic of gender separation comes up in a training, ask practical questions to better understand the problem this strategy is meant to solve.

- If peers are engaging in troubling behavior, consider playing a more active role in building their skills, rather than walking away completely.

- If you are personally sexually harassed, seek the help and support you need while exploring options available to you in your workplace.

TYING IT ALL TOGETHER

In every workplace, diverse perspectives and experiences lie under the surface when it comes to sexual harassment and violence. There are victims of childhood sexual abuse, leaders who believe myths and misperceptions about harassment, social justice advocates eager to call out these myths and misperceptions, and young professionals afraid to ask questions that could end their careers. Navigating these conversations can feel so volatile and scary that we avoid them altogether, to the detriment of our colleagues, friends, and organizations.

Every uncomfortable conversation I engage in with employees, managers, and leaders leaves me feeling optimistic about the future. Silence is powerful. But conversation is culture. When we are empowered to start and sustain conversations about how we relate to each other, the results are nothing short of transformational.

In writing this book, I think about conversations—the stones—that will pave a pathway to a better future. I think about Paul, the COO of a tech company who, inspired by the concept of uncomfortable conversations, challenged himself to have thirty in thirty days. I think about the man in his sixties who leaned over after a talk to tell me about his high school girlfriend, a rape survivor, and wondered aloud whether he said or did the right things. I think about the survivors who have thanked me for bringing their experiences into their workplaces in ways they hadn't yet felt safe to do. I think about the advocates who are tired of constantly bringing up these topics and are so grateful to engage others in the work. I think about the executives who leave a session thinking about their own children, and whether they are raising them with the necessary skills to interact effectively in the workplaces of tomorrow.

Every conversation is a cobblestone on the path toward a better tomorrow. Through conversation, we will help to repair the lives that have been broken by sexual harassment and violence. Through conversation, we will build the skills we need to have healthy, satisfying relationships at work. Through conversation, we will prevent sexual harassment from continuing to take place. Through conversation, we will build organizational cultures of safety and respect. While the work may be uncomfortable by design, it's work that can elicit joy, humor, and deeper connections.

As humans, we're naturally flawed. We are sometimes going to make mistakes and hurt each other. But we can minimize the impact of negative interactions by investing in cultures that prioritize safety, respect, and uncomfortable conversations.

As you embark on your own uncomfortable conversations and lay down more cobblestones on this collective pathway we're building together, I hope you will find the same sense of wonder and power that inspires me on a daily basis.

NOTES

START HERE

1. The phrase *#MeToo* was popularized in 2017 and credited to longtime anti–sexual violence activist Tarana Burke. The #MeToo movement reflects decades of work by a broad range of activists and organizations who have dedicated themselves to improving outcomes for survivors of sexual abuse and assault and preventing sexual violence from taking place.

2. S. G. Smith et al., *National Intimate Partner and Sexual Violence Survey: 2015 Data Brief* (Atlanta, GA: Centers for Disease Control and Prevention, May 2018), 2, https://www.cdc.gov/violenceprevention/pdf/2015data-brief508.pdf (accessed May 3, 2019).

3. "Facts about Sexual Harassment," About EEOC, U.S. Equal Employment Opportunity Commission, https://www.eeoc.gov/eeoc/publications/fs-sex.cfm (accessed March 18, 2019).

4. Chai R. Feldblum and Victoria A. Lipnic (co-chairs), "EEOC Select Task Force on the Study of Harassment in the Workplace" (June 2016), https://www.eeoc.gov/eeoc/task_force/harassment/ (accessed May 3, 2019).

5. Pew Research Center, "Sexual Harassment at Work in the Era of #MeToo" (April 2018), https://www.pewsocialtrends.org/wp-content/uploads/sites/3/2018/04/Pew-Research-Center-Sexual-Harassment-Report-April-2018-FINAL.pdf (accessed May 3, 2019).

6. Smith et al., *National Intimate Partner and Sexual Violence Survey.*

7. S. R. Dube et al., "Long-Term Consequences of Childhood Sexual Abuse by Gender of Victim," *American Journal of Preventive Medicine* 28 (2005): 430–438, http://www.theannainstitute.org/ACE%20folder%20for%20website/37LTCG.pdf (accessed March 2019).

8. Rebecca Stotzer, "Violence against Transgender People: A Review of United States Data," *Aggression and Violent Behavior* 14, no. 3 (May–June 2009): 172, https://www.academia.edu/4513690/Violence_against_transgender_people_A_review_of_United_States_data (accessed May 2019).

9. Amy Edmondson, *The Fearless Organization: Creating Psychological Safety in the Workplace for Learning, Innovation, and Growth* (Hoboken, NJ: John Wiley & Sons, 2019), 25–46.

CHAPTER 1. A SKILLS-BASED APPROACH TO SEXUAL HARASSMENT PREVENTION AND RESPONSE

1. Richard Beckhard and Reuben T. Harris, *Organizational Transitions: Managing Complex Change* (Reading, MA: Addison-Wesley, 1987), 98.

2. Charles Duhigg, *The Power of Habit: Why We Do What We Do in Life and Business* (New York: Random House, 2016), 68–86.

3. "Four Stages of Competence," Wikipedia, https://en.wikipedia.org/wiki/Four_stages_of_competence (accessed May 3, 2019).

4. Iris Bohnet, *What Works: Gender Equality by Design* (Cambridge, MA: Belknap Press of Harvard University Press, 2016), 44–61.

CHAPTER 3. KNOW THE FACTS

1. Chai R. Feldblum and Victoria A. Lipnic (co-chairs), "EEOC Select Task Force on the Study of Harassment in the Workplace" (June 2016), https://www.eeoc.gov/eeoc/task_force/harassment/ (accessed May 3, 2019).

2. E. Shaw et al., "Sexual Harassment and Assault at Work: Understanding the Costs" (Institute for Women's Policy Research, October 2018), https://iwpr.org/wp-content/uploads/2018/10/IWPR-sexual-harassment-brief_FINAL.pdf (accessed May 3, 2019).

3. Feldblum and Lipnic, "EEOC Select Task Force on the Study of Harassment in the Workplace."

4. S. G. Smith et al., *National Intimate Partner and Sexual Violence Survey: 2015 Data Brief* (Atlanta, GA: Centers for Disease Control and Prevention, May 2018), 2, https://www.cdc.gov/violenceprevention/pdf/2015data-brief508.pdf (accessed May 3, 2019).

5. S. R. Dube et al., "Long-Term Consequences of Childhood Sexual Abuse by Gender of Victim," *American Journal of Preventive Medicine* 28 (2005): 430–438, http://www.theannainstitute.org/ACE%20folder%20for%20website/37LTCG.pdf (accessed March 2019).

6. Rebecca Stotzer, "Violence against Transgender People: A Review of United States Data," *Aggression and Violent Behavior* 14, no. 3 (May–June 2009): 172, https://www.academia.edu/4513690/Violence_against_transgender_people_A_review_of_United_States_data (accessed May 2019).

7. M. C. Black et al., "The National Intimate Partner and Sexual Violence Survey (NISVS): 2010 Summary Report" (Atlanta, GA: National Center for Injury Prevention and Control, Centers for Disease Control and Prevention, 2011), 20–21, https://www.cdc.gov/violenceprevention/pdf/NISVS_Report2010-a.pdf (accessed May 2019).

8. Department of Defense, "Fiscal Year 2016 Annual Report on Sexual Assault in the Military" (Washington, D.C.: Department of Defense, 2017), 5, https://www.sapr.mil/public/docs/reports/...Annual/FY16_SAPRO_Annual_Report.pdf (accessed May 2019).

9. Allen J. Beck et al., "Sexual Victimization in Prisons and Jails Reported by Inmates, 2011–2012" (Washington, D.C.: Bureau of Justice Statistics, Department of Justice, 2013), https://www.bjs.gov/content/pub/pdf/svpjri1112.pdf (accessed May 2019).

10. D. Cantor et al., "Report on the AAU Campus Climate Survey on Sexual Assault and Sexual Misconduct" (Rockville, MD: The Association of American Universities, 2015), https://www.aau.edu/sites/default/files

/%40%20Files/Climate%20Survey/AAU_Campus_Climate_Survey_12
_14_15.pdf (accessed May 2019).

11. A. L. Coker et al., "Evaluation of the Green Dot Bystander Approach to
Reduce Interpersonal Violence among College Students across Three Cam-
puses," *Violence against Women* 21, no. 12 (December 2015): 1507–1527, https://
www.researchgate.net/publication/264833180_Evaluation_of_the
_Green_Dot_Bystander_Intervention_to_Reduce_Interpersonal_Violence
_Among_College_Students_Across_Three_Campuses (accessed May 2019).

12. Dube et al., "Long-Term Consequences of Childhood Sexual Abuse by Gender of Victim."

13. J. Boden et al., "Exposure to Childhood Sexual and Physical Abuse and Subsequent Educational Achievement Outcomes," *Child Abuse & Neglect* 31, no. 10
(October 2007): 1101–1114.

14. J. L. Jasinski et al., "The Experience of Violence in the Lives of Homeless
Women: A Research Report (Document No. 211976)," report submitted to
the National Institute of Justice, U.S. Department of Justice (September
2005), http://www.ncjrs.gov/pdffiles1/nij/grants/211976.pdf (accessed
May 2019).

15. M. S. Saar et al., "The Sexual Abuse to Prison Pipeline: The Girls' Story"
(Washington, D.C.: Human Rights Project for Girls, Center on Poverty
and Inequality at Georgetown Law, Ms. Foundation for Women, 2015).

16. Vincent Felitti et al., "Relationship of Childhood Abuse and Household Dys-
function to Many of the Leading Causes of Death in Adults. The Adverse
Childhood Experiences (ACE) Study," *American Journal of Preventive Medicine*
14, no. 4 (1998): 245–258.

17. C. Peterson et al., "Lifetime Economic Burden of Rape among U.S. Adults,"
American Journal of Preventive Medicine 52, no. 6 (2017): 691–701.

18. Shaw et al., "Sexual Harassment and Assault at Work: Understanding the
Costs."

19. Sarah Michal Greathouse et al., *A Review of the Literature on Sexual Assault
Perpetrator Characteristics and Behaviors* (Santa Monica, CA: RAND Corporation, 2015), 7–28, https://www.rand.org/content/dam/rand/pubs/research
_reports/RR1000/RR1082/RAND_RR1082.pdf (accessed May 2019).

20. Feldblum and Lipnic, "EEOC Select Task Force on the Study of Harassment
in the Workplace."

CHAPTER 5. PAUSE THE REACTION

1. See "The Enliven Project: The Truth about False Accusation" at
https://www.sarahbeaulieu.me/the-enliven-project.

2. Dylan Matthews, "The Saddest Graph You'll See Today," *Washington Post*,
January 7, 2013, https://www.washingtonpost.com/news/wonk/wp/2013
/01/07/the-saddest-graph-youll-see-today/?noredirect=on&utm_term
=.c7ac5a15e425.

3. Amanda Marcotte, "This Rape Infographic Is Going Viral. Too Bad It's
Wrong," Slate, January 8, 2013, https://slate.com/human-interest/2013/01

/the-enliven-project-s-false-rape-accusations-infographic-great-intentions
-but-it-isn-t-accurate.html.

4. Chuck Ross, "Rape Statistics. The Anatomy of a Lie," Stop Abusive and
Violent Environments, January 8, 2013, http://www.saveservices.org/2013
/01/rape-statistics-the-anatomy-of-a-lie/.

5. Katie J. M. Baker, "Show This Depressing Graphic to the Rape Apologist in
Your Life," Jezebel, January 7, 2013, https://jezebel.com/show-this-depress
ing-graph-to-the-rape-apologist-in-you-5973904.

CHAPTER 7. SEE THE WHOLE PICTURE

1. Sarah Michal Greathouse et al., *A Review of the Literature on Sexual Assault
Perpetrator Characteristics and Behaviors* (Santa Monica, CA: RAND Corporation, 2015), 7–28, https://www.rand.org/content/dam/rand/pubs
/research_reports/RR1000/RR1082/RAND_RR1082.pdf (accessed May
2019); and Martie Thompson et al., "Trajectories and Predictors of Sexually
Aggressive Behaviors during Emerging Adulthood," *Psychology of Violence* 3,
no. 3 (2013), 247–259, https://www.apa.org/pubs/journals/features/vio-a00
30624.pdf (accessed May 2019).

CHAPTER 9. HELPFUL INTERVENTION

1. A. L. Coker et al., "Evaluation of the Green Dot Bystander Approach to
Reduce Interpersonal Violence among College Students across Three Cam-
puses," *Violence against Women* 21, no. 12 (December 2015): 1507–1527, https://
www.researchgate.net/publication/264833180_Evaluation_of_the_Green
_Dot_Bystander_Intervention_to_Reduce_Interpersonal_Violence_Among
_College_Students_Across_Three_Campuses (accessed May 2019).

2. J. Benner, "Engaging Bystanders to Prevent Sexual Violence: A Guide for
Preventionists" (Enola, PA: National Sexual Violence Resource Center, 2013),
http://www.nsvrc.org/sites/default/files/publications_nsvrc_guide
_engaging-bystanders-prevent-sexual-violence_0.pdf (accessed July 2019).

CHAPTER 11. RESPONDING TO DISCLOSURES
AND SUPPORTING SURVIVORS

1. S. G. Smith et al., *National Intimate Partner and Sexual Violence Survey: 2015 Data
Brief* (Atlanta, GA: Centers for Disease Control and Prevention, May 2018),
2, https://www.cdc.gov/violenceprevention/pdf/2015data-brief508.pdf
(accessed May 3, 2019).

2. S. R. Dube et al., "Long-Term Consequences of Childhood Sexual Abuse
by Gender of Victim," *American Journal of Preventive Medicine* 28 (2005):
430–438, http://www.theannainstitute.org/ACE%20folder%20for%20
website/37LTCG.pdf (accessed March 2019).

3. Rebecca Stotzer, "Violence against Transgender People: A Review of United
States Data," *Aggression and Violent Behavior* 14, no. 3 (May–June 2009): 172,
https://www.academia.edu/4513690/Violence_against_transgender_people
_A_review_of_United_States_data (accessed May 2019).

ACKNOWLEDGMENTS

It is grace that covers the distance between what one person can humanly do and what the world needs to have done. I'm grateful for the grace provided to me by so many people in my life. At the center is my partner and teammate, Marc, and our children, Lucas and Simone. They did what was necessary to make it possible for a wife and mom to lean in hard to this work.

In no particular order, and with too many likely missing, I also want to express gratitude to the following people:

My parents, Judy and Orville Pierson, and brother Paul are a constant presence.

My extended family taught me that I could speak up and survive.

Bright lights in my life: Maryellen Butke, Russ Hammonds, Jody Yen, Miriam Ryvicker, Ariana Jaffe, Victoria Smith, Cara Willis, Liz Kleinerman, Allison Blecker, and Marisol Page.

The athletes and coaches at JP CrossFit who cheered on my AMWAPS, especially Amy Sobota, Jenna Muri-Rosenthal, Cathy Miller, Tim Wells, and the 5 a.m. #PowerUp crew.

The earliest champions of my pursuit of sexual violence prevention in a professional context: Mark Edwards, Kevin Jennings, John Werner, Erin Rubin, Kate Murtagh, and the TEDxBeaconStreet community.

Mentors and spirit guides: Len Schlesinger, Saul Kaplan, Amy Gallo, and Morra Aarons-Mele.

Friends and allies in the sexual violence prevention community: Kim Warnick, Miriam Joelson, Toyin Ajayi, and the staff and board of the Boston Area Rape Crisis Center.

Readers who provided feedback: Joseph Porcelli, Jordan Jozwik, Becky Kennedy, Burt Boltuch, Ben Cohen, and Ye-Seul Kim.

My deepest gratitude—and apologies—for all those whose names I forgot or omitted. I am blessed to have had so many cobblestones on my path that it would be impossible to list them all here by name. I am grateful to the many friends and strangers who participated in this listening and learning journey that has unfolded over the course of my life. Thank you. And let's keep talking.

Finally, as a first-time author, I'm grateful for all the people who took a chance on me. My agent, Jeff Herman, believed in me and this book before the rest of the world cared to talk about sexual violence and harassment. Anna Leinberger, my editor at Berrett-Koehler, showed her passion for this topic and these conversations from the very first time we spoke. And a special shout-out to my dad, an author in his own right, who read multiple drafts and provided countless hours of coaching and support throughout the pitching and writing process, and to my mom, who pored over pages and pages of my careless typos.

accountability: for friend's inappropriate behavior, 172–174; laws on perpetrator, 19, 23; for offensive humor and jokes, 9, 121–122, 173–174; self-assessment on sexual harassment, 38; shame contrasted with, 87; for silence about sexual harassment, 9; whole-picture perspective, 86, 87, 88
Adverse Childhood Experience Study, 47
alcohol/drug use, 4, 85–86, 116, 133, 175
anger: curiosity and open-mindedness replacing, 65–70; justifiable, 68–69, 76
assessment, conversation experience, 34–38

biases, 27
blame: healing deterred with, 74; pausing reaction for, 73–76; shame relation to, 75; of victim, xv
boundaries: case studies and scenarios on, 129–130, 131–132; compliance training lack of focus on, 20; in conversation plan, 160–161; diversity in feelings about, 133–134, 138; with humor and jokes, 132; and physical contact, 79–81, 134–135; policies on, 132–133; power dynamics in negotiating, 133, 138; practice conversations about, 111, 134–137, 138; principles related to, 133; setting and respecting, 129–138, 139; skills, 6, 10, 111, 129–130, 131–135; survey on experience with, 35; uncomfortable conversations revealing, 130–131;

with workplace dating pressures, 136–137
bystander intervention. See intervention

case studies and scenarios: on boundaries, 129–130, 131–132; on experience and expectations of sexual harassment training, 30–31; on intervention, 106–107; men's experience of sexual harassment, 93–97; "My Colleague Was Assaulted and Needs Support," 147–150; "The Naked Mud-Wrestling Video," 106–110; of non-native speakers' experience of sexual harassment, 93–97; about practice conversations, 12, 106–110; on reporting and disclosures, 93–97, 147–150; "Shouldn't This Be Obvious?," 30–31; on support of colleague, 147–150; whole-picture perspective, 95. See also practice conversations
Centers for Disease Control and Prevention, 4, 47
change management, 26–27, 28
child-parent conversations. See parent-child conversations
child sexual abuse: child disclosure to parent about, xiii–xiv, 101; conflicting feelings in personal experience of, 56; by family member, xiii, 56, 92; healing from, xiii–xiv; physical and mental health impacts from, xiv, 47; whole-picture perspective of survivors of, 92
Civil Rights Act of 1964, 4

clients, harassment from. *See* third-party harassment

colleagues: interactions with other gender, 171–172, 177; support of/from, xiv, 114, 123, 147–150

compliance training: boundaries not covered in, 20; concerns after, 19; conversation plan on, 158; human resources department's role in, 22; laws and policies covered in, 18, 19, 21, 28; men's experiences after, 19; reactions and consequences of, 18–20; reporting process covered in, 21–23, 28, 140, 155; skills and support lacking in, 18, 20; as skills-based prevention first step, 21–23, 28; trust issues and, 23

conversation challenges: friends' inappropriate behavior, 172–174, 177; about gender separation in workplace, 171–172, 177; on reporting, 176–177; with self-assessment of behavior, 174–176; on workplace relationships, 170–171, 177

conversation experience: assessment of, 23–24, 32–34, 39; assessment surveys, 11–12, 33–38, 39, 51, 159; case study survey on, 30–31; in conversation plan, 159; discomfort level with, 58, 63; expectations in relation to, 29–30; family impact on, xiii, 31, 32, 36; foreign-language learner's example of, 29–30, 32; about personal feelings and behaviors, 35; range and diversity of, 31–33, 34, 51, 179; on reporting and disclosures, 37–38; in sexual harassment training, 31, 32, 36–37; on social media, 38; with survivors/victims, 32, 35, 36, 37; with transgender survivors, 35, 37; for women, 37. *See also* practice conversations

conversation plan, manager-led: about, 157–158; annual, 164; conversation experience reflection

in, 159; habits and action steps, 163–168; intervention tasks in, 160; policy and process tasks in, 158–159; power and boundaries tasks in, 160–161; practice conversations in, 162; reporting and disclosures addressed in, 159, 161; role of one-on-one conversations in, 157–158; skills development tasks in, 162; support and awareness initiative in, 161; Uncomfortable Conversation Framework tasks in, 159–160

conversations, uncomfortable: boundaries in, 130–131; defining and recognizing, 6–7; empowerment with, 179–180; and fear of negative reaction, 101, 102–103; and gender diversity, 6, 163; group for skills-based approach to, 166–168; habits around, xiii, 157, 163–168; initiation of, 11; obstacles to, 14, 101, 102–103, 116–117; parent-child, xiii–xiv, 8; risk without framework for, 12; role of facts in, 13, 48, 50–52, 96; skills assessment for, 11–12, 23–24, 32–38, 39, 51, 159; social activism aiding skill for, xv–xvi; surveys, 11–12, 33–38, 39, 51, 159; trust forged with, 8; trusting in impact of, 27; value of, 6–8, 163; workplace culture supporting, 27, 163–164. *See also* conversation challenges; discomfort; practice conversations; Uncomfortable Conversation Framework

customers, harassment from. *See* third-party harassment

dating. *See* workplace relationships

disabilities, 126

disclosures. *See* reporting and disclosures

discomfort: conversation experience relation to, 58, 63; diverse origins of, 56–57, 63; embracing, 9–10, 13,

55–58; in intersections of workplace and personal life, 57–58; and language correctness, 58; practice in tolerating, 58; in reporting and disclosures, 55; role of trust issues in, 57; with safety threats, 57; sources of and response to, 55, 59, 60–62 (table), 63; Uncomfortable Conversation Framework and skill for, 13, 55–59, 60–62 (table)
drug use. *See* alcohol/drug use
Duhigg, Charles, 27

EEOC. *See* Equal Employment Opportunity Commission
empathy: practice conversation about, 153–154; with reporting and disclosures, 140–142, 148, 155; for survivors in workplace, 151–154; in whole-picture perspective, 86
empowerment: with reporting and disclosures, 142–143; with uncomfortable conversations, 179–180
Equal Employment Opportunity Commission (EEOC): reporting to, 47, 177; sexual harassment claims in 2017 to, 47; sexual harassment defined under, 4; 2018 report on sexual harassment from, 48–49

facts: myths and misperceptions countered with, 45, 52; necessary, 45–48; open to and critical assessment of, 48–50, 53; opinion discerned from, 50, 53; about perpetrators, 47–48; polarization in media and, 49–50; role in uncomfortable conversations, 13, 48, 50–52, 96; social media misrepresentation of, 70–72; role of, 51–52, 53; in Uncomfortable Conversation Framework, 13, 45–53
family: behavior learned from, xiii, 73; child sexual abuse by, xiii, 56, 92; conversation experience impacted by, xiii, 31, 32, 36

fears: men's experience in relation to, 89–90; #MeToo movement revealing women's, 89, 171; of negative reactions, 101, 102–103; with reporting and disclosures, 46, 147–150
feedback: boundary setting, 130–131; in conversation plan, 158; value of, 72
fertility conversation, 130–131
financial burdens, 47
fraternities, sexual violence in, xv
friends: inappropriate behavior from, 172–174, 177; peer pressure considerations with, 78, 108, 122, 173, 174; support from, xiv, 114, 123, 147–150

gender: and concerns about separation in workplace, 171–172, 177; in demographics of survivors and perpetrators, 48; polarization by, 44, 116; and power dynamics, 125–126; whole-picture perspective of, 89–90, 98
gender diversity: in Uncomfortable Conversation Framework, 44; in workplace culture, 5–6, 10, 26–27
getting help, 15
Giovanni (fictional case study character), 93–97
glossary of terms, 4–5
GreenDot, 46–47
grief, 90–91

habits: active approach in changing, 26, 28, 163–168, 179–180; for individuals/employees, 164–165; for managers, 157, 163–164, 168; resources for forming, 26; role of practice conversations in, 25, 105, 163, 168; of silence, xiii; teamwork in forming, 163, 164; trust and belief role in changing, 27; uncomfortable conversation, xiii, 157, 163–168

healing, xiii–xiv, 57, 74
health impacts, xiv, 47
heterosexuality, 89, 126
hotline numbers, 15
hugging, 79–81
human resources department: conversation group oversight of, 166; in conversation plan, 158; role of, in compliance training, 22; role of, in reporting, 142–143, 144, 146, 147
humor and jokes, 60 (table); accountability in allowing offensive, 9, 121–122, 173–174; boundaries and, 132; in intervention approach, 174; pausing the reaction to, 65–67; practical questions about offensive, 77–78; about sexual harassment training, 19, 121–122

identity oppression, 27
immigrants: and language barrier, 69–70; and sexual harassment, 45, 46. See also non-native speakers
Internet safety, 7–8
intervention: brainstorming for, 109–110, 119–120, 121–122; case studies and scenarios on, 106–107; categories of, 117–118; colleague support for, 114, 123; in conversation plan, 160; humor in, 174; impacts of, 46–47, 115, 117; in jokes about sexual harassment training, 121–122; practice conversations about, 25, 106–109, 111, 119–122, 123; purpose of, understanding, 114–115; signs and behaviors for considering, 115–116; silence in place of, 113–114; skills, 25, 108–109, 111, 118, 165; steps for, 118; strategies for, 111, 117–118, 123; tactics of bystander, 115; third-party evaluation of, 46–47; and whole-picture perspective, 113–114

jokes. See humor and jokes

language: barriers, 69–70; discomfort about appropriate, 58; power with dominant, 126. See also non-native speakers
laws and legal issues, 4, 47; compliance training covering, 18, 19, 21, 28; leaders/managers understanding of, 49; perpetrator accountability, 19, 23; reporting, 147, 177; on sexual harassment definition, 4, 18, 49; on support, 111, 140, 144. See also workplace policies

managers and leaders: expectations of, for sexual harassment training, 30–31; habits and action steps for, 157, 163–164, 168; power inherent for, 126; third-party harassment response from, 127–128; trust in reporting to, 139–140; understanding laws and policies, 49. See also conversation plan, manager-led; reporting and disclosures
Matthews, Dylan, 70
men: cultural norms for women contrasted with, 89–90; and discussion of sexual violence, xv; experience of compliance training, 19; fear response toward, 89–90; intimacy challenges for, xv; and #MeToo movement, 65–67, 77–79, 171; polarization of, 44, 116; power dynamics, 125–126; sexual harassment in industries dominated by, 45; and workplace interactions with women, 5, 171
men as survivors/victims, 5, 47, 74–75, 76; case study of, 93–97
mental health, xiv, 47
#MeToo movement: men's response to, 65–67, 77–79, 171; proliferation of, 45; women's fear revealed in, 89, 171; workplace culture influenced by, 3, 10, 65–67, 77–79; workplace safety and, 11, 171

National Sexual Assault Hotline, 15
Native Americans, 46
non-native speakers: pausing reactions with, 69–70; sexual harassment experienced by, case study, 93–97

open-mindedness, 65–70, 48–50, 53
optimism, xiv, 179–180

parent-child conversations, xiii–xiv, 7–8, 36, 101
peer pressure, 78, 108, 122, 173, 174
perpetrators, 19, 20, 23, 115; facts about, 47–48; whole-picture treatment of, 87–88; women as, 93–97
perspective. See whole-picture perspective
Pew Research Center study, 5
physical contact: and boundaries, 79–81, 134–135; practice conversation on, 134–135; sexual violence without, 4; survivors' responses to, 151
polarization: facts understood in era of, 49–50; gender, 44, 116; Uncomfortable Conversation Framework contrasted with, 44, 52; whole-picture view compared with, 86–87
policies. See compliance training; workplace policies
pornography, 7–8
power dynamics: in boundary negotiations, 133, 138; compliance training addressing, 19; in conversation plan, 160–161; relation of gender to, 125–126; intervention strategies and, 111; with managers and leaders, 126; practice conversations unveiling, 25, 109, 111; with race and ethnicity, 126; recognizing and addressing, 125–129, 139; in workplace relationships, 169–170

practical questions. See questions, practical
practice: discomfort, 58; habits changed with, 25, 105, 163, 168
practice conversations: approach to, 105; about boundaries, 111, 134–137, 138; case study about, 12, 106–110; and creating habits, 105; empathy and, 153–154; group assessment prior to, 23; about inappropriate jokes and humor, 121–122; on intervention, 25, 106–109, 111, 119–122, 123; mindset for, 9, 11; obstacles avoided with, 101–104, 112; policy clarity with, 105, 149; power dynamics unveiled with, 25, 109, 111; practical questions as form of, 81; prevention impacted with, 25, 28, 150; reactions tempered with, 101–102, 103–104; about reporting and disclosures, 25, 96, 97, 106–109, 127–128, 145–146, 148–150, 155; Sample Nine-Week Manager-Led Conversation Plan, 158–162; skill assessment in, 23–24, 105; in skills-based approach, 25, 28; skills gained with, 110–112; about support, 111, 153–154; about third-party sexual harassment, 127–128; Uncomfortable Conversation Framework relation to, 25, 110, 112; value of, 12, 14, 101–102, 103–107; about workplace dating pressures, 145–146; Practice Conversation #1: Inappropriate Comments, 119–120; Practice Conversation #2: Not Taking Training Seriously, 121–122; Practice Conversation #3: Power Dynamics and Harassment, 127–128; Practice Conversation #4: Display of Affection, 134–135; Practice Conversation #5: Unclear Boundaries and Communication, 136–137; Practice Conversation #6: Obstacles to Reporting, 145–146;

Practice Conversation #7: Survivors at Work, 153–154
prevention and response: common questions regarding, 14; compliance training as first step in, 21–23, 28; habit-forming activities for, 26, 28, 163–168, 179–180; and impact of practice conversations, 25, 28, 150; impact of silence on, 10, 19, 20, 57, 114–115; intervention role in, 46–47, 115, 117; long-term approach to, 33–34; one-size-fits-all as obstacle to, 11, 33, 80, 105; rules contrasted with skills-based approach to, 17–20; skills-based approach to, 11, 17–26, 28; Uncomfortable Conversation Framework role in, 13, 24–25, 28; uncomfortable conversations skill assessment role in, 23–24

questions, practical: art of asking, 13, 79–82; defining, 77–79, 84; about gender separation, 171–172, 177; about hugging, 80–81; about humor and jokes, 77–78; negative reaction to, 82–83, 84; as practice conversation form, 81; purpose of, 77, 84; support aided by, 78–79; in Uncomfortable Conversation Framework, 13, 77–84

race and ethnicity: power dynamics in relation to, 126; sexual violence relation to, 46. *See also* immigrants; non-native speakers
RAND Corporation, 47
rape, social media incident about, 70–72
rape crisis center, xiv, xv–xvi, 74–75
reactions: to compliance training, 18–20; defensive, 75–76; fear of negative, 101, 102–103; feedback gained from, 72; of male survivors, 74–75, 76; origins of, 72, 73;
to practical questions, 82–83, 84; practice conversations tempering, 101–102, 103–104; to shame, 75, 76

reactions, pausing: appropriate role of anger in, 68–69, 76; benefit of, 13, 65, 76; to blame, 73–76; curiosity and open-mindedness replacing anger in, 65–70; with non-native speakers, 69–70; to offensive humor and jokes, 65–67; process of, 69–70; social media blowback and, 70–72; in Uncomfortable Conversation Framework, 13, 65–76

relationships. *See* colleagues; family; workplace relationships
reporting and disclosures: anonymous, 144; case studies and scenarios on, 93–97, 147–150; compliance training covering, 21–23, 28, 140, 155; conversation challenges on, 176–177; conversation experience on, 37–38; conversation plan on, 159, 161; discomfort in, 55; to EEOC, 47, 177; empathy with, 140–142, 148, 155; empowerment with, 142–143; fears and hesitation with, 46, 147–150; human resources department role in, 142–143, 144, 146, 147; on inappropriate dating pressures, 136–137, 145–146; issues impacting, 144, 147; knowledge base importance in, 143, 147; laws and legal issues, 147, 177; mandatory, 128, 144, 149; obstacles to, 46, 145–146; options for, 176–177; policies on, 21–23, 144, 147, 155, 161; practice conversations about, 25, 96, 97, 106–109, 127–128, 145–146, 148–150, 155; understanding process of, 144; rates of failure to, 46; receiving, 143; responding to, 139–143; after sexual harassment workshop, 93–97; supporting, 147–150, 176–177; survey on

experience with, 37–38; trust in, 139–141, 150, 176. *See also* intervention

resilience, xiv, xvi, 93

resources: for habit-building, 26; support, 15, 143, 149–150, 158, 164; for surveys, 39; workplace posting of, 164, 165

rules: perpetrators' disregard for, 19; skills-based approach compared to, 17–20

safety: Internet, 7–8; #MeToo movement and workplace, 11, 171; travel, 125–126, 131, 152; workplace culture encouragement of, xvi, 3, 6, 11, 27, 152, 155, 180

self-assessment, 11–12, 38, 174–176

self-care, 16, 159

sex education, 7–8

sexual abuse and assault, defining, 5

sexual harassment: accountability for silence about, 9; awareness initiative, 161, 164; defining, 4, 5, 18, 49; discomfort embraced in conversations about, 9–10, 13, 55–58; EEOC 2017 claims of, 47; EEOC report on addressing, 48–49; financial burden of claims, 47; freedom from, 5–6; health impacts from, xiv, 47; for immigrants, 45, 46; legal definition of, 4, 18, 49; in male-dominated industries, 45; men's experience of, case study, 93–97; myths and misperceptions of, 45, 52; organization-wide impacts of, 114, 123, 151–153; prevalence and frequency of, 45–46; rates of, 4, 5, 45; self-assessment about, 174–176; silence sustaining culture of, 10, 19, 20, 57, 114–115; spectrum of, 123; survivor/victim terminology with, 5; whole-picture perspective of incident of, 85–88, 98. *See also specific topics*

sexual harassment training: conversation experience with, 31, 32, 36–37; disclosure conversation after, case study, 93–97; expectations of, 29–30; expectations and realities of, case study, 30–31; joking about, 19, 121–122; survey on experience with, 31, 36–37. *See also* compliance training

sexual misconduct, defining, 5

sexual violence: alcohol/drug use with, 4; awareness initiative, 161, 164; conditions that permit, 15; defining, 4, 5; in fraternities, xv; health impacts from, xiv, 47; men's response to discussion of, xv; myths and misperceptions of, 45, 52; noncontact acts of, 4; organization-wide impacts of, 151–153; physical and mental health impacts from, xiv, 47; race and ethnicity in relation to, 46; rates for men as survivors, 5; rates for transgender survivors, 5, 46; rates for women as survivors, 5, 46; survivor/victim terminology with, 5. *See also specific topics*

shame: accountability contrasted with, 87; reactions to, 75, 76; role of blame in, 75

skills: assessment of, 11–12, 23–24, 32–38, 39, 51, 159; boundary, 6, 10, 111, 129–130, 131–135; compliance training lacking focus on, 18, 20; development of, 110–112, 162; intervention, 25, 108–109, 111, 165; practice conversations revealing, 23–24, 105; and social activism, xv–xvi; Uncomfortable Conversation Framework and discomfort, 13, 55–59, 60–62 (table)

skills-based approach: compliance training as first step of, 21–23, 28; conversation experience assessment in, 23–24, 32–34, 39; conversation group for, 166–168;

habit-building activities in, 26, 28, 167–168; practice conversations in, 25, 28; to prevention and response, 11, 17–26, 28; questions about, 14; rationale behind, 26–27; versus rules, 17–20; soccer analogy for, 17–18; step-by-step outline for, 20–26, 28; teamwork in, 26; Uncomfortable Conversation Framework in, 24–25, 28

social activism: inspiration for, xiv–xv; uncomfortable conversation skills gained in, xv–xvi

social media: conversation experience on, 38; rape graphic blowback on, 70–72

support: action steps in showing, 159, 161, 165, 166, 167–168; case study on colleague, 147–150; after child sexual abuse, xiv; compliance training lacking coverage of, 18, 20; conversation plan on, 161; from friends and colleagues, xiv, 114, 123, 147–150; laws and legal issues on, 111, 140, 144; listening and presence in, xiv, 78–79, 92; practical questions in, 78–79; practice conversations about, 111, 153–154; reporting and disclosure, 147–150, 176–177; resources for, 15, 143, 149–150, 158; role of facts in, 51–52, 53; with sexual assault awareness initiative, 161, 164; for transgender individuals, 35, 37; for unhealthy behaviors, 176; whole-picture perspective with, 92–93, 98; workplace culture friendly to, 3, 25, 27, 151–154, 163–164, 165, 180

surveys: on boundaries, 35; conversation experience assessment, 11–12, 33–38, 39, 51, 159; conversation experience case study, 30–31; critical assessment of, 50; EEOC, 49; on reporting and disclosure experience, 37–38; resources for, 39; sample introduction for, 34; on

sexual harassment training experience, 31, 36–37; uncomfortable conversation skills, 11–12, 33–38, 39, 51, 159

survivors/victims: of child sexual abuse, xiii–xiv, 47, 56, 92, 101; conversation experience with/about, 32, 35, 36, 37; empathy for workplace, 151–154; gender in demographics of, 48; health impacts for, xiv, 47; male, reactions for, 74–75, 76; physical contact for, 151; prevalence in workplace, 15; sexual violence rates for, 5, 46; silence of others impacting, 10, 57; solidarity of, 15; stereotypes about, 44; terminology clarification, 5; uniqueness of experiences of, 15–16; whole-picture perspective of, 90–93, 98; workplace policies conflicting with wishes of, 149. See also men as survivors/victims; support; women as survivors/victims

teamwork: conversation assessment significance in, 33, 39; conversation group, 166–168; for habit-forming, 163, 164; in skills-based approach, 26; think-pair-share, 160–161. See also conversation plan, manager-led

therapy, 166

third-party harassment, 49, 113–114; policies about, 147; practice conversation about, 127–128

training. See compliance training; conversation plan, manager-led; sexual harassment training

transgender individuals: sexual violence rates for, 5, 46; supporting, 35, 37

travel safety, 125–126, 131, 152

trust: building, 8, 102, 105, 120, 139–140, 152; compliance training and, 23; discomfort in relation to, 57; in

reporting and disclosures, 139–141, 150, 176; in uncomfortable conversation, 27; violations of, 74
Tumblr, 70–72

Uncomfortable Conversation Framework: background of, 43–45, 52; benefits of, 8, 13, 14, 24–25; case study exemplifying, 93–97; in conversation plan, 159–160; discomfort and, 13, 55–59, 60–62 (table); facts in, 13, 45–53; gender-inclusivity of, 44; as mindset, 44; overview of, 12, 13; pausing reaction in, 13, 65–76; polarized frameworks compared with common, 44, 52; practical questions in, 13, 77–84; and practice conversations, 25, 110, 112; in prevention and response, 13, 24–25, 28; in skills-based approach, 24–25, 28; value of, 44–45, 52, 102; whole-picture perspective in, 13, 85–93, 95, 98
uncomfortable conversations. See conversations, uncomfortable; discomfort

victim-blaming, xv
victims. See survivors/victims
videos in workplace, offensive, 106–110

whole-picture perspective: of accountability, 86, 87, 88; case study exemplifying, 95; empathy in, 86; of gender roles, 89–90, 98; of incident, 85–88, 98; intervention aided by, 113–114; in perpetrator treatment, 87–88; polarized view contrasted with, 86–87; of survivors' lives, 90–93, 98; in Uncomfortable Conversation Framework, 13, 85–93, 95, 98
women: conversation experience for, 37; cultural norms for men contrasted with, 89–90; men challenged by workplace interac-

tions with, 5, 171; men's intimacy challenges with, xv; and #MeToo movement, 89, 171; as perpetrators of sexual harassment, 93–97; polarization of, 44, 116; power dynamics for men compared to, 125–126
women as survivors/victims, 5, 46, 47. See also #MeToo movement
workplace culture: building trust, 102, 105, 120, 139–140, 152; changing management vision for, 26–27, 28; gender-diverse, 5–6, 10, 26–27; hugging in, 79–81; intersection with personal life, 57–58; #MeToo movement influence on, 3, 10, 65–67, 77–79; resilience in, xvi; safety encouraged in, xvi, 3, 6, 11, 27, 152, 155, 180; sexual harassment-free, 5–6; sexual harassment impacts on, 114, 123, 151–153; support-friendly, 3, 25, 27, 151–154, 163–164, 165, 180; uncomfortable conversations encouraged in, 27, 163–164; volatile, 5–6. See also sexual harassment
workplace policies: in boundary setting, 132–133; compliance training covering, 18, 19, 21, 28; in conversation plan, 158–159; knowledge of, 49, 94–94, 164–165; managers understanding, 49; on office relationships, 170, 177; practice conversations clarifying, 105, 149; reporting, 21–23, 144, 147, 155, 161; third-party harassment, 147; for travel safety, 125–126, 131, 152; victim wishes compared with, 149. See also compliance training
workplace relationships: conversation challenges about, 170–171, 177; power dynamics in, 169–170; practice conversations about, 145–146; reporting inappropriate pressure for, 136–137, 145–146; workplace policies on, 170, 177

ABOUT THE AUTHOR

Sarah Beaulieu is a speaker and consultant who trains workplaces and advises leaders on skills-based sexual harassment prevention and response. Her expertise has been featured in multiple news outlets, including Fox News, *Harvard Business Review*, the Associated Press, the U.S. Chamber of Commerce, NPR, AskMen, and the *Boston Business Journal*. In 2018, Sarah, along with Russ Hammonds, co-founded *An Uncomfortable Conversation*, a nonprofit YouTube channel that helps people engage in meaningful conversations about sexual violence through short videos. A proud graduate of Brown University, Sarah lives in Boston, Massachusetts, with her family.

Berrett–Koehler
BK Publishers

Berrett-Koehler is an independent publisher dedicated to an ambitious mission: *Connecting people and ideas to create a world that works for all.*

Our publications span many formats, including print, digital, audio, and video. We also offer online resources, training, and gatherings. And we will continue expanding our products and services to advance our mission.

We believe that the solutions to the world's problems will come from all of us, working at all levels: in our society, in our organizations, and in our own lives. Our publications and resources offer pathways to creating a more just, equitable, and sustainable society. They help people make their organizations more humane, democratic, diverse, and effective (and we don't think there's any contradiction there). And they guide people in creating positive change in their own lives and aligning their personal practices with their aspirations for a better world.

And we strive to practice what we preach through what we call "The BK Way." At the core of this approach is *stewardship,* a deep sense of responsibility to administer the company for the benefit of all of our stakeholder groups, including authors, customers, employees, investors, service providers, sales partners, and the communities and environment around us. Everything we do is built around stewardship and our other core values of *quality, partnership, inclusion,* and *sustainability.*

This is why Berrett-Koehler is the first book publishing company to be both a B Corporation (a rigorous certification) and a benefit corporation (a for-profit legal status), which together require us to adhere to the highest standards for corporate, social, and environmental performance. And it is why we have instituted many pioneering practices (which you can learn about at www.bkconnection.com), including the Berrett-Koehler Constitution, the Bill of Rights and Responsibilities for BK Authors, and our unique Author Days.

We are grateful to our readers, authors, and other friends who are supporting our mission. We ask you to share with us examples of how BK publications and resources are making a difference in your lives, organizations, and communities at www.bkconnection.com/impact.

Dear reader,

Thank you for picking up this book and welcome to the worldwide BK community! You're joining a special group of people who have come together to create positive change in their lives, organizations, and communities.

What's BK all about?

Our mission is to connect people and ideas to create a world that works for all.

Why? Our communities, organizations, and lives get bogged down by old paradigms of self-interest, exclusion, hierarchy, and privilege. But we believe that can change. That's why we seek the leading experts on these challenges—and share their actionable ideas with you.

A welcome gift

To help you get started, we'd like to offer you a **free copy** of one of our bestselling ebooks:

www.bkconnection.com/welcome

When you claim your **free ebook**, you'll also be subscribed to our blog.

Our freshest insights

Access the best new tools and ideas for leaders at all levels on our blog at ideas.bkconnection.com.

Sincerely,

Your friends at Berrett-Koehler

Certified

Corporation